ATTACHMENT THEORY

A GUIDE TO BOWLBIAN PSYCHOLOGY

TABLE OF CONTENTS

INTRODUCTION TO ATTACHMENT THEORY

Preliminary Considerations

Attachment theory, developed by John Bowlby and later expanded upon by Mary Ainsworth, provides foundational insights into the complex dynamics of parent-child relationships and has significantly influenced the field of developmental psychology and beyond. At its core, this theory seeks to understand how early experiences with caregivers shape an individual's emotional and social development. The concept of attachment encompasses the emotional bond that forms between an infant and their primary caregiver, typically the mother, and how this bond influences the child's sense of security, exploration, and relationships throughout their life. Central to the theory is the idea that a secure attachment with a caregiver provides a safe haven for the child to explore the world, knowing they can return to a source of comfort and support when needed. Conversely, insecure attachments can lead to difficulties in regulating emotions, forming healthy relationships, and coping with stress. Attachment theory also delves into the behavioral and neurological aspects of human bonding, shedding light on the mechanisms underlying trust, empathy, and intimacy. As we delve deeper into the core principles and concepts of attachment theory, it becomes evident that the quality of early attachments plays a crucial role in shaping one's internal working models of self and others, which can impact various aspects of adult functioning, including parenting styles, romantic relationships, and mental health outcomes. Furthermore, the theory emphasizes the importance of recognizing the diversity of attachment experiences and patterns, acknowledging that individual differences exist within secure, anxious, and avoidant attachment categories. Understanding attachment theory can offer valuable insights for professionals working in fields such as clinical psychology, education, and family therapy, as well as inform interventions and support systems for individuals and families managing challenges related to attachment insecurity. By exploring the overarching framework of attachment theory, we begin to grasp the profound implications of early relational experiences, paving the way for a deeper understanding of human connections and emotional well-being.

Definition, Core Principles and Concepts

At its core, attachment pertains to the emotional bond individuals form with their primary caregivers, serving as a blueprint for future relationships and influencing social and emotional functioning throughout the lifespan. Key principles and concepts within the framework of attachment theory encompass the notion of a secure base, internal working models, and the role of proximity-seeking behavior in response to perceived threats or distress. These ideals underpin the foundation of attachment theory, elucidating the nature of human connections and the impact of attachment experiences on various aspects of an individual's life.

The concept of a 'secure base' represents the foundation from which individuals explore the world and seek comfort during times of uncertainty or distress. From infancy to adulthood, this secure base is often personified by the primary caregiver and remains instrumental in facilitating exploration, providing a sense of safety, and fostering emotional regulation. Additionally, the development of internal working models, influenced by early attachment experiences, encapsulates cognitive schemas that dictate one's expectations of relationships, perceived self-worth, and trust in others. These internal representations shape how individuals interpret social cues, manage conflicts, and establish intimacy, exerting a profound influence on their relational patterns. Moreover, proximity-seeking behavior, manifested through expressions of distress or efforts to maintain closeness with attachment figures, serves as a primal instinct aimed at ensuring protection and security, further delineating the fundamental tenets of attachment theory.

As we delve deeper into the core principles and concepts of attachment theory, it becomes evident that the implications extend far beyond infancy and childhood, permeating into adolescence and adulthood. Understanding these foundational principles fosters insight into the complexities of human relationships, emphasizing the impact of early attachment experiences on emotional well-being and interpersonal dynamics. Furthermore, recognizing the interplay of these concepts offers a lens through which to comprehend individual differences in attachment styles, coping strategies, and resilience in the face of adversity.

Significance in Human Development

Attachment theory plays a crucial role in shaping our understanding of human development, particularly in the formative years of childhood. It is through the lens of attachment that we can comprehend the profound impact of early experiences on an individual's emotional and psychological well-being. The significance of attachment in human development lies in its foundational influence on the formation of social bonds, emotional regulation, and personality traits. Early attachment relationships serve as the blueprint for how individuals perceive and engage with the world, laying the groundwork for future interpersonal connections and coping strategies. Moreover, the quality of early attachments has been linked to various aspects of mental health, including resilience, self-esteem, and the ability to cope with stress and adversity. These formative attachments set the stage for the development of a person's internal working models – cognitive frameworks that shape perceptions of self and others, guiding behavior in relationships throughout the lifespan. Understanding the significance of attachment in human development underscores the critical role of caregivers in fostering secure attachments. Responsive and sensitive caregiving provides a sense of security and trust, enabling children to explore their environment and develop a secure base from which to engage with the world. Conversely, disruptions in attachment, such as neglect or inconsistent care, can have lasting repercussions, potentially leading to attachment insecurities and difficulties in forming healthy relationships. The significance of attachment in human development extends beyond childhood, influencing one's capacity for intimacy, empathy, and overall well-being in adult life.

The Role of Early Relationships in Attachment Formation

The quality of caregiving experienced in infancy and early childhood sets the stage for the establishment of attachment patterns that can endure throughout life. Bowlby's attachment theory emphasizes the critical impact of early relationships on an individual's emotional and social functioning. Infants form their first attachments with primary caregivers, usually the mother or father, and the nature of these early interactions profoundly shapes their internal working models of relationships.

During the formative stages of life, infants rely on their caregivers not only for physical needs but also for emotional support and security. Caregivers who are attuned and responsive to the infant's cues foster a sense of trust and safety, laying the foundation for secure attachment. In contrast, inconsistent or neglectful caregiving can engender insecure attachment patterns characterized by anxiety, ambivalence, or avoidance in intimate relationships later in life.

Attachment formation is intrinsically linked to the development of self-regulation and coping mechanisms. Securely attached individuals tend to exhibit greater emotional resilience and adaptive coping strategies, while insecurely attached individuals may struggle with regulating their emotions and addressing stressors effectively. Studies have demonstrated that early relational experiences shape the neural circuitry involved in emotion regulation, making early attachment experiences a fundamental aspect of personality development.

Early attachment dynamics impact an individual's expectations of relationships and influences their interpersonal behaviors. Children who experience consistent responsive caregiving tend to develop positive beliefs about themselves and others, fostering healthy relationship dynamics in adulthood. Conversely, individuals with insecure attachment may struggle with intimacy, trust, and communication, often experiencing difficulties in forming and maintaining close relationships.

Understanding the profound impact of early relationships on attachment formation highlights the importance of providing adequate support and resources for caregivers and families. Interventions aimed at promoting secure attachment, such as parent education programs and early childhood interventions, can mitigate the negative effects of adverse early experiences and foster healthy relationship patterns for future generations. By recognizing the significance of early relationships in shaping attachment, professionals in various fields can contribute to nurturing resilient and emotionally healthy individuals within society.

Attachment Theory and Its Impact on Personality

Attachment theory has been instrumental in shaping our understanding of personality development and its implications in human behavior. As proposed by John Bowlby and further elaborated upon by Mary Ainsworth, this theory posits that early experiences with caregivers significantly influence the formation of an individual's personality. The type of attachment style established during infancy, whether secure, anxious, or avoidant, can have profound and lasting effects on various aspects of an individual's personality. Moreover, these attachment patterns serve as a blueprint for how individuals perceive themselves, their relationships with others, and their ability to regulate emotions.

Researchers have found that individuals with secure attachment tend to exhibit traits such as resilience, self-confidence, and effective emotion regulation. They are more likely to form healthy and satisfying interpersonal relationships, demonstrating empathy, trust, and intimacy. Conversely, individuals with insecure attachment, whether characterized by anxiety or avoidance, may display maladaptive personality traits, including difficulty in forming close relationships, fear of intimacy, and heightened emotional reactivity. These individuals may also struggle with low self-esteem, a negative self-concept, and challenges in managing stress.

In addition to shaping interpersonal dynamics, attachment theory also sheds light on the development of specific personality traits and behavioral patterns. For instance, individuals with a secure attachment style often demonstrate a greater openness to new experiences, increased emotional intelligence, and a more positive outlook on life. On the other hand, those with insecure attachment may exhibit traits like dependency, mistrust, and a tendency towards emotional volatility. Furthermore, attachment theory offers insights into the formation of coping mechanisms, defense mechanisms, and adaptability in response to stress and adversity.

Understanding the impact of attachment on personality is crucial in various domains, including clinical psychology, counseling, and social work. Mental health professionals leverage this knowledge to tailor interventions that address underlying attachment-related issues and promote healthy personality development. By recognizing the influence of early attachment experiences, therapists can help individuals manage their interpersonal challenges and cultivate greater self-awareness and emotional resilience.

Behavioral Systems in Attachment Theory

Behavioral systems encompass a range of adaptive strategies and behaviors that individuals employ to manage their social environment and establish and maintain interpersonal relationships. These systems are deeply intertwined with attachment processes and significantly contribute to an individual's overall attachment style.

One of the core behavioral systems within attachment theory is the caregiving system, which pertains to nurturing, protecting, and providing for others, particularly in the context of caregiving responsibilities towards offspring or significant others. This system not only influences a person's capacity for empathy and responsiveness but also plays a crucial role in shaping their caregiving behaviors. Moreover, the exploration of the caregiving system unravels the complex web of influences that impact an individual's ability to form secure attachments and engage in nurturing relationships.

Conversely, the attachment behavioral system embodies the intrinsic need for proximity and support from attachment figures, serving as the driving force behind seeking comfort, reassurance, and security in times of distress or uncertainty. It entails behaviors and strategies aimed at establishing and maintaining connection and closeness with primary attachment figures, thereby fostering feelings of safety and emotional well-being. A deep comprehension of the attachment behavioral system facilitates an in-depth analysis of attachment patterns and reactions, shedding light on the underlying motivations behind an individual's attachment-related behaviors and responses.

The exploration of exploratory behavior and the formation of peer relations elucidates the significance of sociability, curiosity, and interaction in the development of attachment bonds and interpersonal connections. This system encompasses the innate drive for exploration, social engagement, and the cultivation of peer relationships, showcasing how these factors intertwine with attachment processes to shape an individual's social and emotional development. Understanding the manifestations and implications of exploratory behavior offers valuable insights into the multifaceted nature of attachment and its profound impact on an individual's social integration and adaptability.

Modern Relevance and Applications of Attachment In Understanding Human Behavior

Attachment theory has, over the years, proven to be highly relevant in understanding human behavior across various contexts. One of the key modern applications of attachment theory lies in its connection with mental health outcomes. Numerous empirical studies have established a strong association between early attachment experiences and an individual's psychological well-being throughout their lifespan. Individuals who have formed secure attachments in infancy exhibit greater emotional regulation, higher self-esteem, and better interpersonal relationships in adulthood. On the contrary, insecure attachments have been linked to increased susceptibility to anxiety, depression, and personality disorders. This insight has significantly influenced the field of clinical psychology, where practitioners leverage attachment theory to inform therapeutic interventions and treatment approaches. Moreover, the relevance of attachment theory extends beyond clinical settings and into broader societal implications. An individual's attachment style can impact their behavior in educational, professional, and social environments. Understanding one's attachment style can provide valuable insights into their approach to learning, decision-making, leadership, and conflict resolution. Organizations and institutions are increasingly recognizing the significance of attachment theory in shaping group dynamics, team collaboration, and organizational culture. In the context of parenting and childcare, attachment theory has revolutionized caregiving practices by emphasizing the importance of responsive and sensitive interactions between caregivers and children. This paradigm shift has laid the foundation for attachment-based parenting strategies that prioritize the emotional needs of children and promote secure attachment bonds. Furthermore, attachment theory has demonstrated its relevance in diverse cultural contexts, highlighting universal patterns of attachment behaviors while acknowledging cultural variations in caregiving practices and attachment norms. The adaptability and universality of attachment theory make it a robust framework for understanding human behavior across different societies.

Common Myths about Attachment Theory

One of the common myths surrounding attachment theory is that it implies that parents must be perfect in order to foster secure attachment in their children. This misconception often leads to feelings of guilt and inadequacy among parents who may believe that any misstep in caregiving will have long-lasting negative effects on their child's attachment security. However, attachment theory acknowledges that caregivers do not need to be flawless;

rather, it underscores the importance of providing consistent, sensitive, and responsive care as the foundation for healthy attachment relationships.

Another prevalent myth is that attachment patterns are set in stone during infancy and cannot be changed later in life. This deterministic view undermines the potential for individuals to develop and internalize secure attachment styles through therapeutic interventions, supportive relationships, and self-awareness. Research has shown that individuals can indeed modify their attachment behaviors and form more secure attachments through intervention programs and personal growth.

Additionally, some misconceptions suggest that attachment theory only applies to parent-child relationships, disregarding its relevance to adult romantic partnerships, friendships, and professional interactions. Contrary to this belief, attachment theory posits that the core principles of attachment – such as seeking proximity, feeling secure, and regulating emotions – extend to all interpersonal relationships across the lifespan. Understanding these dynamics can inform interventions and strategies for enhancing relational well-being in diverse contexts.

It is also mistakenly assumed that attachment theory blames parents or caregivers for any attachment insecurities experienced by individuals. However, attachment theory emphasizes the role of early experiences and the caregiving environment in shaping attachment patterns, without assigning blame or fault to specific individuals. Rather than focusing on attributions of blame, attachment theory encourages a compassionate understanding of how early experiences influence attachment styles and promotes supportive interventions to facilitate secure attachments.

Finally, a common misunderstanding is that attachment theory ignores individual differences and diversity in attachment patterns, leading to oversimplified categorizations. In actuality, attachment theory recognizes the complexity and variability of attachment experiences, allowing for diverse expressions of attachment behavior influenced by cultural, social, and personal factors. Acknowledging this diversity strengthens the theory's capacity to encompass and address the nuances of attachment dynamics across different populations and contexts.

Comparisons with Other Psychological Theories

In examining Attachment Theory, it is vital to contrast its concepts and postulates with other prevailing psychological theories to elucidate its distinguishing features and contributions to the field of psychology. Notably, one prominent comparison lies in contrasting Attachment Theory with psychodynamic theories, particularly those developed by Sigmund Freud. While Freudian theories emphasize the role of unconscious motives and drives, Attachment Theory focuses on the formation and impact of interpersonal relationships, specifically within the context of early caregiving experiences. This distinction underscores an inherent emphasis on social bonds and emotional connections within Attachment Theory, offering a comprehensive understanding of human behavior. Additionally, when juxtaposed with cognitive theories such as Piaget's theory of cognitive development, Attachment Theory demonstrates its unique focus on the socio-emotional domain, highlighting the significance of emotional security and caregiver responsiveness in shaping an individual's cognitive and emotional development. Moreover, comparative analysis with behavioral theories reveals that while both perspectives acknowledge the influence of environmental factors, Attachment Theory places a particular emphasis on the quality of interpersonal relationships and their impact on an individual's psychological well-being. Furthermore, the intersection of Attachment Theory with contemporary evolutionary psychology elucidates the adaptive functions and survival value of attachment behaviors. This interdisciplinary perspective emphasizes how attachment patterns serve as biological mechanisms that facilitate proximity maintenance and protection, underscoring the crucial role of attachment processes in evolutionary fitness. Importantly, these comparisons underscore the unique characteristics of Attachment Theory and its integrative approach to understanding human behavior, drawing from diverse psychological paradigms while emphasizing the impact of early relationships on individuals' psychological and emotional development.

HISTORICAL CONTEXT AND DEVELOPMENT

Psychoanalytic Influences

In the field of developmental psychology, the influence of psychoanalytic theories was profound in laying the groundwork for the emergence of modern attachment theory. The pioneering works of Sigmund Freud, particularly his emphasis on the significance of early childhood experiences and the mother-child relationship, served as a precursor to the later formulation of attachment theory. Freud's conceptualizations of infantile sexuality, the unconscious mind, and the impact of early life experiences on psychological development created a fertile foundation for scholars and researchers to delve into the intricacies of attachment dynamics. Moreover, the work of influential psychoanalysts such as Melanie Klein and Donald Winnicott further enriched the discourse on early relational experiences and their impact on personality formation. Klein's concept of the 'internal working model' and Winnicott's theories of maternal provision and holding environment significantly contributed to the evolving understanding of attachment processes and caregiver-infant interactions. Their ideas foreshadowed the core tenets of attachment theory, providing impetus for subsequent empirical investigations and theoretical advancements. By examining the familial and environmental influences on emotional development, psychoanalytic thinkers paved the way for the transition from instinct-driven explanations to a more comprehensive understanding of the socio-emotional dimensions of human bonding.

The Role of Ethology in Shaping Attachment Theory

Ethology, a field of study that focuses on the behavior of living organisms in their natural environments, played a crucial role in shaping the foundation of attachment theory. Groundbreaking work by ethologists such as Konrad Lorenz and Nikolaas Tinbergen provided significant insights into the behavior of animals and its relevance to human behavior, which greatly influenced the development of attachment theory. Lorenz's studies on imprinting in geese, for instance, highlighted the innate nature of certain attachment behaviors and laid the groundwork for understanding the critical period in human infant attachment. This concept was later incorporated into John Bowlby's attachment theory, emphasizing the importance of early bonding and its impact on later social and emotional development. Tinbergen's research on fixed action patterns and releasers also contributed to the understanding of instinctual behaviors and their role in human attachment. This ethological perspective provided a valuable framework for understanding the adaptive function of attachment behaviors and their evolutionary significance. Furthermore, ethological observations of animal maternal care and offspring interactions provided parallels for understanding human caregiving and attachment dynamics. These comparative studies helped researchers recognize universal patterns of attachment across different species, reinforcing the idea that attachment is a fundamental aspect of biological and psychological development. The ethological approach also underscored the significance of the environment in shaping attachment behaviors, shedding light on the interplay between genetic predispositions and environmental influences. By integrating ethological principles, attachment theory transcended traditional psychological frameworks and offered a more comprehensive understanding of human attachment as a product of both biological and environmental factors. This interdisciplinary approach enriched the theoretical foundation of attachment theory, contributing to its widespread influence in developmental psychology and related fields. In essence, the role of ethology in shaping attachment theory not only provided essential empirical support but also broadened the scope of inquiry, ultimately establishing attachment theory as a pivotal framework for understanding human social and emotional development.

Observational Studies - Mother and Child Interactions

Observational studies have played a pivotal role in unraveling the intricacies of mother-child interactions and their profound impact on attachment formation. One seminal study by Mary Ainsworth and her colleagues at the University of Virginia's Child Development Center pioneered the 'Strange Situation' experiment, which provided a structured framework for evaluating infant attachment patterns. This groundbreaking methodology revolutionized the understanding of maternal sensitivity, infant responsiveness, and the development of secure and insecure attachment styles. Moreover, it elucidated the crucial role of a caregiver's availability and responsiveness in shaping a child's sense of security and exploration. The use of observational paradigms has further revealed the bidirectional nature of mother-child interactions, emphasizing how children actively contribute to the establishment of attachment bonds through cues, signals, and expressions of needs. These studies have underscored the significance of non-verbal communication, such as touch, gaze, and proximity, in fostering a secure base for the infant's exploration of the surrounding environment. Furthermore, longitudinal observational research has highlighted the effects of early mother-child interactions on later social and emotional development, emphasizing the continuity of attachment across the lifespan. By meticulously capturing the dynamics of these interactions, researchers have been able to discern the nuanced differences between secure, anxious, and avoidant attachment patterns, providing invaluable insights into the developmental trajectories of children. As technology and interdisciplinary collaborations continue to advance, observational studies are leveraging innovative methods, such as neuroimaging and physiological measures, to deepen our understanding of the neural mechanisms underpinning attachment processes.

Transition from Behavioral Theories to Attachment Constructs

During the mid-20th century, a significant shift occurred in the field of psychology, particularly in the domain of child development and social behavior. This transition marked a pivotal turning point, as behavioral theories of conditioning and reinforcement gave way to a more holistic and nuanced understanding of human attachment and bonding. The evolution from behaviorism to attachment constructs signified a departure from viewing interpersonal relationships as mere products of learned responses, to recognizing the profound influence of emotional connections and caregiving experiences on individual development.

The prevailing behaviorist paradigms, championed by psychologists such as B.F. Skinner, emphasized the role of environmental stimuli in shaping observable behaviors. While these principles undoubtedly contributed to our understanding of learning and acquisition of specific actions, they fell short in capturing the dynamics of human affection, trust, and security in relationships. It became evident that traditional behaviorist models were insufficient in elucidating the complexities of attachment formation and its enduring effects across the lifespan.

Amidst this backdrop, pioneering researchers and scholars, including John Bowlby, Mary Ainsworth, and Harry Harlow, spearheaded a transformative reimagining of human bonds. Central to this paradigm shift was the recognition of innate biological predispositions and the significance of early caregiver-child interactions in shaping emotional well-being. Theoretical tenets from ethology, psychoanalysis, and cognitive psychology converged to provide a more comprehensive framework for comprehending attachment processes. The emphasis moved from purely external reinforcements to internal working models and internal representations of relationships – key elements that underpin attachment theory.

The realization that infants and young children actively seek proximity to their caregivers not just for physical needs but also for emotional security underscored the inadequacy of behaviorist explanations alone. The transition from behavioral theories to attachment constructs thus encompassed a fundamental shift in perspective – from behavior modification to acknowledging the inherent human need for connection and bonding. This shift laid the foundation for a more holistic understanding of human development.

Research and Experiments

Pioneering studies conducted by researchers such as Mary Ainsworth, Harry Harlow, and Konrad Lorenz have provided invaluable insights into the nature and impact of early attachments. One of the most influential pieces of research in this domain is Ainsworth's 'Strange Situation' study, which classified infant attachment into different categories: secure, insecure-avoidant, and insecure-ambivalent/resistant. This seminal work laid the foundation for further exploration of attachment patterns and their implications for later development. Harry Harlow's studies on infant rhesus monkeys demonstrated the profound effects of social isolation and maternal deprivation on emotional and social functioning, emphasizing the critical role of caregiving and nurturing in healthy psychological development. Additionally, Konrad Lorenz's research on imprinting in geese and ducks shed light on the instinctual processes underlying the formation of early bonds, highlighting the evolutionary significance of attachment behaviors. In addition to these classic studies, contemporary research using advanced methodologies such as neuroimaging and longitudinal assessments has deepened our understanding of the neural mechanisms underpinning attachment and the long-term outcomes associated with early relational experiences. Furthermore, experimental studies exploring the effects of interventions aimed at enhancing parental sensitivity and responsiveness have demonstrated the potential for positive changes in attachment security and overall child well-being. The culmination of these groundbreaking research efforts has expanded the scope of attachment theory, guiding clinical practice and policymaking related to child welfare and family support.

Influence of World War II on Child-Care Practices and Attachment

World War II had a profound impact on child-care practices and subsequently, on the development of attachment theory. The widespread upheaval caused by the war led to significant changes in family dynamics, as many fathers were enlisted in military service, leaving mothers to assume the role of primary caregivers. This shift in caregiving responsibilities prompted researchers to investigate the effects of maternal separation on infant and child development. Studies conducted during and after the war, such as those by René Spitz and John Bowlby, provided critical insights into the adverse consequences of prolonged separations and institutional rearing on children's emotional and psychological well-being.

The observations made during this period highlighted the detrimental effects of inadequate or disrupted parental care, laying the groundwork for understanding the importance of consistent and responsive caregiving in fostering secure attachments. The wartime context also spurred interest in the mechanisms by which children formed emotional bonds with their caregivers amid adversity, shedding light on the evolution of attachment behaviors as adaptive responses to challenging environments.

The experiences of war or displacement prompted scholars to explore the implications of trauma and loss on children's attachment patterns. These investigations paved the way for recognizing the complex interplay between early experiences, environmental influences, and long-term socioemotional development. Notably, research conducted during and after World War II played a pivotal role in shaping the theoretical tenets of attachment theory, underscoring the significance of the caregiver-child relationship in mitigating the adverse effects of stress and instability.

The aftermath of the war also catalyzed discussions on societal attitudes towards child-rearing practices and the broader implications for familial and community support systems. Scholars and practitioners began advocating for policies and interventions aimed at promoting secure attachments and addressing the emotional needs of children affected by the tumultuous wartime conditions.

Integration with Cognitive and Psychodynamic Perspectives

Cognitive psychology, with its focus on mental processes such as perception, attention, memory, and problem-solving, has provided valuable insights into the mechanisms underlying attachment-related behaviors. From a cognitive perspective, attachment styles can be viewed as internal working models that shape individuals' expectations about themselves and others in relationships. These mental representations influence how individuals perceive and interpret social cues, which in turn affect their attachment-related behaviors. Furthermore, cognitive theories have elucidated the role of attribution processes in shaping attachment patterns, highlighting the impact of individuals' subjective interpretations of interpersonal experiences. The intersection of attachment theory with cognitive psychology has thus shed light on the cognitive processes that underpin the formation, maintenance, and modification of attachment bonds.

On the other hand, the integration of attachment theory with psychodynamic perspectives, rooted in the traditions of psychoanalysis, has deepened our understanding of the emotional and unconscious dimensions of attachment. Central to the psychodynamic perspective is the notion of unconscious drives and conflicts influencing human behavior and relationships. Psychodynamic theories have underscored the significance of early childhood experiences, particularly parent-child interactions, in shaping individuals' emotional development and attachment patterns. By exploring the unconscious motivations and unresolved conflicts that underlie attachment dynamics, psychodynamic perspectives have illuminated the interplay between past experiences, intrapsychic processes, and present relational patterns. Moreover, the concept of transference, a key construct in psychodynamic theory, has been applied to understand the reenactment of early attachment relationships in adult interpersonal contexts. This lens has offered valuable insights into how past attachment experiences continue to reverberate in adult relationships, shaping individuals' emotional responses and relational dynamics.

Emergence of Key Figures and Collaborations

During the evolution of attachment theory, numerous researchers and clinicians played pivotal roles in shaping and refining its core concepts. One such influential figure is Mary Ainsworth, whose extensive work on maternal sensitivity, infant-mother interactions, and the development of the Strange Situation procedure made substantial advancements in our understanding of attachment patterns. Ainsworth's groundbreaking research not only provided empirical evidence for the classification of attachment styles but also paved the way for subsequent studies on the impact of secure attachment on child development.

Another prominent figure in the history of attachment theory is Mary Main, whose development of the Adult Attachment Interview (AAI) expanded the scope of attachment research to encompass adult relationships and their early attachment experiences. Main's contributions facilitated the exploration of how childhood attachment patterns manifest in adult interpersonal relationships, shedding light on the continuity of attachment across the lifespan.

Collaborative efforts within the field of attachment theory have also been instrumental in advancing our understanding of human relationships. The collaboration between John Bowlby and psychiatrist James Robertson resulted in seminal studies on the effects of maternal separation and the significance of caregiver presence in promoting secure attachment. This partnership underscored the importance of observational research in elucidating the dynamics of attachment and laid the groundwork for subsequent studies examining the impact of early experiences on later social and emotional functioning.

The interdisciplinary collaboration between attachment theorists, neuroscientists, and developmental psychologists has yielded valuable insights into the neurological underpinnings of attachment processes. Through the integration of neurobiological findings with attachment principles, researchers have gained a more comprehensive understanding of how early relational experiences shape brain development and influence socioemotional functioning.

The Establishment of Attachment Theory as a Cornerstone of Developmental Psychology

Attachment theory has had a profound impact on various domains of psychology, including child development, social psychology, and clinical practice. Central to this influence is the notion that early experiences with primary caregivers play a critical role in shaping an individual's emotional and social development throughout the lifespan. The significance of attachment theory is underscored by its enduring relevance and applicability. It provides a powerful lens through which to examine the intricacies of human relationships, caregiving dynamics, and emotional wellbeing. Furthermore, the theoretical tenets of attachment have not only enriched our comprehension of normal development but have also informed therapeutic interventions for individuals experiencing relational or emotional difficulties, thereby illustrating its practical utility. The prevalence and impact of attachment theory on diverse areas of psychology affirm its status as an indispensable pillar of developmental inquiry. Through empirical research and clinical observations, attachment theory has yielded valuable insights into the mechanisms underlying interpersonal bonds, the effects of early adversity on psychological functioning, and the adaptive strategies individuals employ to manage social connections. By elucidating the nature of attachment patterns and their implications for mental health, attachment theory has significantly advanced our grasp of human behavior and emotional regulation. Moreover, its integration with neurobiological findings has shed light on the neurodevelopmental underpinnings of attachment processes, offering a comprehensive understanding of the interplay between biology and environment in shaping human attachment.

JOHN BOWLBY AND THE GENESIS OF ATTACHMENT STUDIES

Early Life and Influences

Born in London in 1907 into an influential and intellectual family, John Bowlby's upbringing provided him with a rich environment that nurtured his curiosity about human behavior and relationships. His father, Sir Anthony Bowlby, was a renowned surgeon, while his mother, May Bowlby, hailed from a family of social reformers and activists. This combination of medical and humanitarian influences undoubtedly played a role in shaping Bowlby's multifaceted approach to understanding the complexities of human attachment.

Bowlby's early education at prestigious institutions such as Trinity College, Cambridge, exposed him to a diverse array of intellectual pursuits. While studying preclinical sciences, he gravitated toward subjects that integrated aspects of biology, psychology, and anthropology, laying the groundwork for his interdisciplinary approach to later psychological research. The burgeoning fields of ethology and psychoanalysis caught his attention, providing him with insights into the fundamental nature of human bonding and emotional development.

On the other hand, Bowlby's exposure to the works of Sigmund Freud and other prominent psychologists during his academic years deeply influenced his philosophical orientation toward the study of human behavior. The interplay between nature and nurture, as well as the significance of early experiences in shaping individual personalities, became recurring themes in his subsequent scholarly endeavors. Furthermore, Bowlby's engagement with the emerging concept of environmental determinism sparked his interest in investigating how early childhood experiences impact adult mental health and social functioning.

His formative years were also marked by frequent interactions with individuals from various cultural backgrounds, thanks to his family's involvement in philanthropy and public service. These encounters broadened his perspective on human relationships and fortified his commitment to understanding the universal elements of attachment across different societies. It is evident that Bowlby's early life experiences, coupled with his eclectic academic journey, paved the way for his groundbreaking theories on attachment and human development.

Academic Background and Training

Bowlby's earliest exposure to the field of psychology occurred during his undergraduate years at Trinity College, Cambridge. His studies in natural sciences allowed him to delve into various disciplines, including biology, psychology, and ethology. This multidisciplinary approach not only honed his analytical skills but also kindled an early interest in the intersection of human behavior and evolutionary principles.

After completing his undergraduate degree, Bowlby embarked on further academic pursuits, earning a medical degree from University College Hospital in London. His medical training instilled in him a deep understanding of human physiology and the complexities of mental health, providing a substantial foundation for his later contributions to developmental psychology. It was during this period that Bowlby began to integrate his medical knowledge with psychological theories, laying the groundwork for his groundbreaking research on attachment.

Additionally, Bowlby's early professional experiences greatly enriched his academic development. His work in child psychiatry exposed him to the profound impact of early relationships on children's emotional well-being, fostering a keen interest in delving deeper into the mechanisms underlying these formative bonds. This practical exposure further fueled his resolve to bridge the gap between clinical observation and theoretical constructs, propelling him towards a more holistic and encompassing approach to understanding human attachment.

Bowlby's immersion in the British Psychoanalytic Society provided him with invaluable insights into the prevailing psychoanalytic theories of the time. Engaging with prominent figures in the field broadened his perspective and encouraged critical reflection on existing paradigms of human development and behavior. These exchanges would ultimately inform his departure from traditional psychoanalytic views, culminating in the formulation of his pioneering attachment theory.

Initial Forays into Developmental Psychology

After completing his academic training, John Bowlby embarked on a remarkable journey into developmental psychology that would forever change the landscape of psychological research. His early experiences as a medical student at the University of Cambridge and subsequent psychoanalytic training under the guidance of Melanie Klein laid the groundwork for his future contributions to the field. Bowlby's keen interest in the emotional development of children led him to critically examine the prevailing models of human attachment and maternal deprivation. This exploratory phase marked the beginning of a lifelong quest to unravel the complexities of human relationships and their impact on emotional well-being.

In his initial forays into developmental psychology, Bowlby delved into the emerging theories of ethology, particularly the work of Konrad Lorenz. The study of animal behavior provided invaluable insights into the biological and evolutionary underpinnings of human attachment, nurturing Bowlby's pioneering concept of the innate attachment behavioral system. Drawing inspiration from ethological studies, Bowlby recognized the universal nature of attachment behaviors across different species, laying the groundwork for his groundbreaking theory.

During this formative period, Bowlby sought to bridge the gap between psychoanalysis and empirical research, thereby advocating for a more interdisciplinary approach to understanding human behavior. His engagement with diverse fields such as evolutionary biology, cognitive psychology, and social anthropology exemplified his commitment to developing a holistic framework for comprehending attachment dynamics. This integrative approach set the stage for a paradigm shift in developmental psychology, fostering an appreciation for the multifaceted influences that shape attachment patterns.

Bowlby's early exploration into the sphere of developmental psychology underscored his enduring curiosity and intellectual rigor. Through a meticulous review of existing literature and the synthesis of disparate disciplines, he began to crystallize the fundamental tenets of attachment theory. The amalgamation of theoretical constructs, empirical evidence, and clinical observations propelled Bowlby to reevaluate conventional notions of parenting, maternal care, and child development.

Collaboration with Mary Ainsworth

John Bowlby's collaboration with Mary Ainsworth marked a pivotal moment in the history of attachment studies. Ainsworth, an American-Canadian developmental psychologist, shared Bowlby's passion for understanding the dynamics of parent-child relationships and their impact on human development. The synergy between their expertise and research interests led to groundbreaking contributions to the field of attachment theory. Their partnership was characterized by a shared commitment to empirical research and a deep understanding of the complexities of early bonding. Together, they pioneered innovative methodologies that revolutionized the assessment of attachment patterns in infants and young children.

Ainsworth's 'Strange Situation' experiment, conducted in collaboration with Bowlby, significantly advanced the understanding of infant-caregiver attachment dynamics. This seminal study provided valuable insights into the nature of secure and insecure attachment, laying the foundation for the classification of attachment styles that continue to influence clinical and developmental psychology today. Their collaborative efforts also resulted in the formulation of the concept of the 'secure base,' which emphasized the role of caregivers in providing a secure anchor for exploration and emotional support.

Beyond their research endeavors, Bowlby and Ainsworth's collaboration extended to the dissemination of their findings through publications and academic presentations. Their joint publications, including influential papers and books, established a comprehensive framework for understanding attachment behaviors and their long-term implications. Through their collective efforts, they effectively challenged prevailing misconceptions about child rearing and the significance of early experiences in shaping individuals' socioemotional development.

The legacy of Bowlby and Ainsworth's collaboration lies in their reciprocal mentorship and the cultivation of a vibrant academic community dedicated to advancing attachment theory. Their collaborative spirit fostered an environment where diverse perspectives were welcomed, leading to enriched theoretical insights and methodological innovations. Scholars and practitioners across the globe continue to draw inspiration from the seamless synergy that characterized Bowlby and Ainsworth's partnership, perpetuating their profound impact on attachment research and clinical practice.

Formulation of Attachment Theory

John Bowlby's formulation of Attachment Theory marked a significant milestone in the field of developmental psychology. At its core, the theory sought to elucidate and understand the nature of the bond formed between infants and their primary caregivers, focusing on how these early relationships shape and influence an individual's socioemotional development. Drawing from various disciplines such as ethology, evolutionary biology, and psychoanalysis, Bowlby proposed a framework that underscored the fundamental importance of secure attachment in laying the foundation for healthy psychological functioning and interpersonal relationships throughout one's lifespan.

Central to the theory was the concept of the 'attachment behavioral system,' a biologically rooted set of behaviors and responses that evolved to ensure the survival and protection of the young. Bowlby postulated that this innate system operates as a proximity-seeking mechanism, compelling infants to seek closeness and contact with their attachment figures in times of distress or discomfort. Moreover, he emphasized that the quality of care and responsiveness provided by the caregiver profoundly influences the development of internal working models, which serve as cognitive representations guiding future social interactions and the formation of subsequent relationships.

An essential tenet of Bowlby's theory was the identification of four distinct attachment styles: secure, anxious-ambivalent, anxious-avoidant, and disorganized. Through longitudinal studies and observational research, Bowlby and his collaborators, notably Mary Ainsworth, conducted the pioneering 'strange situation' experiments to empirically investigate these attachment patterns and their implications for child development. The insights gleaned from these studies provided empirical support for the existence of secure base phenomena, wherein securely attached infants utilized their caregiver as a source of comfort and exploration of the environment, while insecurely attached infants exhibited varying degrees of distress and disengagement.

In developing his theory, Bowlby also underscored the critical role of parental sensitivity and responsiveness in fostering secure attachment. He contended that sensitive caregiving, characterized by prompt, contingent, and emotionally attuned responses to the infant's cues, forms the cornerstone for nurturing secure attachments. Furthermore, Bowlby extended the applicability of attachment theory beyond infancy, proposing that these early attachment experiences continue to exert an impact on subsequent romantic relationships, friendships, and even the individual's capacity for emotional regulation and coping with adversity.

Studies and Experiments

John Bowlby's groundbreaking studies and experiments in the field of attachment theory revolutionized our understanding of early childhood development and parent-child relationships. His extensive research laid the foundation for numerous psychological inquiries into the nature of human attachment, leading to profound insights that continue to influence contemporary studies. Bowlby's seminal work centered on comprehending the mechanisms and dynamics of attachment formation, exploring the impact of early experiences on emotional and behavioral patterns, and delving into the long-term consequences of attachment styles. One of the most influential studies conducted by Bowlby was the '44 thieves study,' which investigated the correlation between maternal deprivation and delinquency. This pioneering research highlighted the critical role of a secure attachment in mitigating antisocial behavior, thereby prompting significant advancements in the fields of child welfare and psychology. In addition to empirical studies, Bowlby's innovative experiments, such as the 'strange situation' assessment developed in collaboration with Mary Ainsworth, provided invaluable insights into infant-caregiver relationships and attachment classifications. These experiments not only elucidated the distinct attachment patterns – secure, anxious-ambivalent, avoidant, and disorganized – but also underscored the influence of early interactions on an individual's socioemotional development. Furthermore, through longitudinal studies tracking the trajectories of children with different attachment orientations, Bowlby demonstrated how secure attachments engendered resilience, while insecure attachments often precipitated psychological and social difficulties. The meticulous methodology and ethical considerations employed in Bowlby's studies set a gold standard for future research in developmental psychology, cementing his status as a trailblazer in the field. By fostering greater awareness of the pivotal role of early bonding experiences, Bowlby's studies and experiments have significantly shaped therapeutic interventions, parental guidance practices, and institutional policies aimed at promoting healthy attachments and nurturing environments for children. Indeed, the impact of Bowlby's pioneering studies and experiments reverberates through the continued integration of attachment theory into diverse domains, from education and mental health to social work and public policy.

Impact on Child and Family Welfare Policies

By shedding light on the pivotal role of early caregiver-child relationships in shaping lifelong emotional and behavioral patterns, Bowlby's theories paved the way for policy initiatives aimed at nurturing secure attachments within families. Governments and organizations worldwide have incorporated Bowlby's insights into their child welfare frameworks, recognizing the importance of stable, loving environments for optimal child development. In particular, attachment theory has informed foster care and adoption practices, emphasizing the need for continuity and stability in children's placements to facilitate healthy attachment bonds.

Additionally, Bowlby's work has influenced family support programs, highlighting the significance of parental sensitivity and responsiveness in promoting secure attachments. Interventions focused on enhancing parental caregiving skills and strengthening parent-child relationships have been shaped by attachment theory, aiming to prevent adverse childhood experiences and support positive developmental outcomes. Moreover, the understanding of attachment-related issues such as separation anxiety and reactive attachment disorder has informed therapeutic and support services for at-risk children and families, guiding tailored interventions to address underlying attachment disruptions.

Attachment theory has underscored the critical importance of early intervention and preventative measures in mitigating the long-term effects of insecure attachments on children's well-being. This awareness has led to the integration of attachment-informed practices in early childhood education, mental health services, and social work, fostering holistic approaches that prioritize attachment security and emotional resilience. Moreover, policy efforts focusing on parental leave, childcare provisions, and family-friendly workplace policies have drawn inspiration from attachment principles, aiming to support parental bonding, reduce stressors, and promote healthy parent-child relationships.

Criticism and Revisions to the Original Theory

The seminal work of John Bowlby and his formulation of attachment theory has not been without its share of criticisms and subsequent revisions. One noteworthy critique concerns the potential cultural bias inherent in some of the early studies that formed the foundation of attachment theory. Critics argue that certain attachment behaviors may be interpreted differently across various cultural contexts, thereby raising questions about the universality of the theory's assumptions.

Scholars have raised concerns about the original model's focus on the mother-child relationship as the primary determinant of a child's attachment patterns. This narrow emphasis on maternal care has been criticized for overlooking the contributions of other caregivers and the broader socio-ecological factors shaping a child's attachment style. As a result, contemporary researchers have sought to expand the scope of attachment theory to encompass diverse familial structures and caregiving dynamics beyond traditional nuclear families.

Another area of contention pertains to the terminology and classification of attachment styles. Some researchers argue that the original tripartite classification of secure, anxious, and avoidant attachment overlooks the complexities and fluidity of attachment behaviors. Over time, revised conceptualizations and additional attachment dimensions such as disorganized or ambivalent attachment have been proposed to better capture the nuanced variations in attachment relationships.

In response to these criticisms, scholars have also endeavored to integrate attachment theory with other theoretical frameworks to enhance its explanatory power. For instance, the intersection of attachment theory with neurobiological research has provided valuable insights into the underlying mechanisms of attachment formation and its impact on emotional regulation and psychopathology. This interdisciplinary approach allows for a more comprehensive understanding of attachment dynamics while addressing some of the limitations identified in the original theory.

Recent efforts have focused on extending attachment theory beyond childhood and adolescence to adulthood, exploring the continuity of attachment patterns and their implications for romantic relationships and mental health outcomes. By examining attachment processes across the lifespan, researchers have enriched the theoretical framework and shed light on the impact of early attachment experiences on adult functioning.

Legacy and Recognition in Modern Psychology

In modern psychology, the legacy of John Bowlby and his attachment theory is profoundly ingrained in both theoretical frameworks and practical applications. Bowlby's pioneering work has left an indelible mark on the understanding of human development, shaping contemporary research and offering invaluable insights into the nature of human relationships. The legacy of Bowlby's attachment theory can be discerned across various domains of psychology, from clinical practice to social and developmental psychology.

One of the foremost legacies of John Bowlby lies in the paradigm shift he initiated in the way psychologists perceive early childhood experiences and their impact on later life. By elucidating the significance of secure attachments in infancy as a foundation for healthy emotional and interpersonal functioning, Bowlby fundamentally altered the landscape of developmental psychology. Furthermore, by highlighting the inherent human need for proximity-seeking behaviors and secure base formation, Bowlby's theory propelled a deeper understanding of the dynamics of human bonding, nurturing, and attachment throughout the lifespan.

Recognition of Bowlby's transformative contributions extends beyond academia and permeates professional fields such as social work, counseling, and psychotherapy. Mental health practitioners routinely draw from Bowlby's attachment theory to comprehend and address relational challenges, trauma, and emotional disturbances experienced by individuals across diverse age groups. The therapeutic applications of attachment theory have proven instrumental in informing interventions aimed at fostering secure attachments in children, addressing attachment disruptions in adults, and cultivating healthier parent-child interactions.

The profound recognition of Bowlby's work is underscored by its integration into public policy initiatives and child welfare practices. Governments, advocacy organizations, and child welfare agencies have embraced the foundational tenets of attachment theory to advocate for policies and programs that prioritize the creation and preservation of secure attachment environments for children and families. This acknowledgement further attests to the substantive impact of Bowlby's legacy on promoting social and familial well-being on a broader societal scale.

In the domain of empirical research, Bowlby's influence remains palpable through an extensive body of scholarship dedicated to investigating the nuanced dimensions of attachment dynamics and their implications. Contemporary researchers continue to build upon Bowlby's theoretical framework, employing sophisticated methodologies to explore the interplay between early attachments and subsequent socio-emotional outcomes. Additionally, interdisciplinary collaborations have further advanced the application of attachment theory to diverse contexts, encompassing neurobiological, cross-cultural, and intergenerational perspectives.

Influence on Contemporary Research

Over the decades, John Bowlby's groundbreaking work in attachment theory has continued to cast a profound influence on contemporary research in psychology, sociology, and related fields. One area where Bowlby's theories continue to be influential is in the study of adult attachment patterns and their implications for romantic relationships and well-being. Researchers have utilized Bowlby's ideas to develop frameworks for understanding how early attachment experiences shape individuals' abilities to form and maintain intimate partnerships in adulthood. By investigating the links between attachment styles and relationship satisfaction, as well as the role of attachment in conflict resolution and emotional regulation, contemporary scholars have expanded upon Bowlby's original insights and shed light on the significance of attachment across the lifespan.

The application of attachment theory to diverse cultural contexts has been an increasingly salient focus of contemporary research. Recognizing that attachment dynamics may manifest differently in various sociocultural environments, researchers have examined how cultural norms, practices, and values intersect with attachment processes. This nuanced approach not only enriches our understanding of attachment dynamics beyond Western populations but also highlights the necessity of considering cultural diversity in psychological research and clinical practice. Bowlby's emphasis on the universality of attachment needs has thus spurred a rich vein of inquiry into the interplay between attachment and cultural factors.

Contemporary research has delved into the neurobiological underpinnings of attachment, drawing on advances in neuroscience to illuminate the neural mechanisms involved in bonding, caregiving, and emotional regulation. By integrating insights from neuroimaging studies, genetic research, and psychophysiological assessments, investigators have elucidated the interplay between genetic predispositions, early experiences, and brain functioning in shaping attachment outcomes.

KEY CONCEPTS AND POSTULATES OF ATTACHMENT THEORY

The Bio-Behavioral System and Its Roots in Evolution

1. Introduction:

The bio-behavioral system represents a fundamental aspect of human development and functioning, particularly in the context of attachment. It encompasses a complex interplay of biological, behavioral, and psychological processes that contribute to our understanding of attachment behaviors and relationships. At its core, the bio-behavioral system involves the coordination between physiological responses, cognitive interpretations, and relational dynamics. Understanding this system is vital for comprehending the mechanisms underlying our attachment-related behaviors and their evolutionary significance.

One of the primary components of the bio-behavioral system is the physiological aspect, which necessitates an exploration of the bodily processes that underpin attachment behaviors. These processes encompass hormonal regulation, neural activation, and sensory perception, all of which influence our emotional experiences and interpersonal connections. For instance, the release of oxytocin, often referred to as the 'bonding hormone,' plays a crucial role in facilitating attachment-related behaviors and promoting feelings of trust and security. Furthermore, the functioning of key brain regions, such as the amygdala and prefrontal cortex, significantly influences our responses to attachment-related stimuli and our ability to form and maintain meaningful relationships.

In addition to its biological underpinnings, the bio-behavioral system involves a behavioral component that encompasses observable actions and interactions within attachment relationships. This facet encompasses a diverse range of behaviors, including proximity seeking, exploration, and responsiveness to distress signals, all of which serve to promote and maintain social bonds. By examining these behaviors through an evolutionary lens, we gain insight into their adaptive functions and their relevance to our ancestors' survival and reproductive success. Moreover, the study of behavioral patterns within attachment relationships provides valuable information about the development and maintenance of secure attachments across the lifespan.

The psychological dimensions of the bio-behavioral system offer a unique perspective on how cognitive processes influence attachment-related behaviors and experiences. Internal working models, which represent cognitive schemas derived from past attachment experiences, significantly shape our expectations and behaviors in current and future relationships. Exploring the formation and modifiability of these internal representations sheds light on the ways in which individuals perceive themselves, others, and relationships, thereby influencing the quality and dynamics of attachment bonds.

2. Historical Perspectives on Evolutionary Psychology:

The study of evolutionary psychology provides a fascinating avenue for exploring the origins and development of human behavior. Dating back to the works of Charles Darwin and William James, the historical perspective on evolutionary psychology traces the evolution of thought and the foundational principles that have shaped our understanding of human nature. The emergence of evolutionary psychology as a distinct field gained momentum in the late 20th century, with influential figures such as Donald Symons, Leda Cosmides, and John Tooby contributing significantly to its development.

One pivotal aspect of historical perspectives on evolutionary psychology is the integration of evolutionary theory into the discipline of psychology, illuminating the adaptive functions and mechanisms that underpin human behavior. By acknowledging the selective pressures and reproductive challenges faced by our ancestors, evolutionary psychology offers valuable insights into the complexities of human cognition, emotions, and social interactions. The notable paradigm shift toward understanding the human mind as a product of natural selection has heralded a profound reevaluation of traditional psychological frameworks.

Historical perspectives encompass the exploration of universal human behaviors and traits as products of evolutionary adaptations. This approach emphasizes the ancestral environment as a crucible for shaping psychological mechanisms, shedding light on the recurrent patterns of behavior and cognitive strategies observed across diverse cultures. Key milestones in the historical narrative include the elucidation of evolutionary roots in kin selection, mating strategies, and parental investment, unveiling the evolutionary underpinnings of complex social dynamics and interpersonal relationships.

The historical trajectory also encompasses the integration of evolutionary psychology with other disciplines, fostering interdisciplinary collaborations that have enriched our understanding of human nature. Contributions from fields such as anthropology, ethology, and genetics have converged to form a comprehensive framework for investigating the evolutionary origins of human behavior. Moreover, the historical evolution of methodologies and empirical approaches within evolutionary psychology has spurred rigorous scientific inquiry, enabling researchers to adeptly address the complexities of human behavior within an evolutionary context.

3. Natural Selection and Attachment - The Darwinian Framework:

The theory of natural selection, proposed by Charles Darwin, forms the cornerstone of modern evolutionary psychology. From an attachment perspective, the Darwinian framework provides valuable insights into the origins and adaptive functions of attachment behaviors. According to this framework, individuals within a species exhibit variation in traits, and those with advantageous traits have a survival and reproductive advantage, leading to the propagation of their genes in successive generations. This process ultimately shapes the behavioral, cognitive, and emotional predispositions related to attachment. In the context of attachment theory, the Darwinian framework illuminates how attachment behaviors and systems have evolved as strategies to enhance survival and reproductive success. To understand this, it is essential to assess the role of attachment-related behaviors in the context of environmental challenges, danger, and care provision among ancestral populations. By examining the survival advantages conferred by attachment-related behaviors, we gain insight into the persistence and refinement of such behaviors across human evolution. Additionally, the Darwinian framework prompts an exploration of the ecological and social contexts that favored the development of specific attachment strategies, shedding light on the interplay between environmental pressures and the emergence of attachment patterns. Furthermore, this framework encourages an examination of the heritability of attachment-related traits, underscoring the genetic basis of these behaviors and drawing attention to the transmission of attachment patterns across generations. Importantly, natural selection also underscores the importance of reproductive fitness and mate selection in shaping attachment dynamics. Understanding the principles of natural selection in the context of attachment theory enriches our comprehension of the adaptive functions, cross-cultural variations, and individual differences in attachment behaviors. Moreover, it imparts a deeper appreciation of the interconnections between evolution, behavior, and attachment, laying a foundation for further exploration and understanding of attachment processes in diverse human populations.

4. Comparative Studies of Primates and Other Species:

The study of attachment in primates and other animal species has been instrumental in shedding light on the evolutionary origins and adaptive functions of attachment behaviors. By observing and comparing the social dynamics and behavioral patterns of various primate species, researchers have gained valuable insights into the nature of attachment across different evolutionary lineages. One of the most influential figures in this field is renowned primatologist, Frans de Waal, whose extensive work on the social behavior of bonobos and chimpanzees has provided crucial evidence for the presence of attachment-like bonds in non-human primates. De Waal's studies, along with those of other primatologists such as Jane Goodall and Dian Fossey, have demonstrated the complex and nuanced nature of social relationships among primates, including affiliative behaviors, cooperation, reconciliation, and even forms of caregiving. Additionally, comparative research has extended beyond primates to encompass a diverse range of animal species, revealing similarities and variations in attachment-related behaviors. For instance, ethological studies have explored the bonding and caregiving behaviors exhibited by various birds, such as swans and penguins, as well as mammals like elephants and dolphins. These investigations have showcased the diverse ways in which attachment systems manifest in different ecological and phylogenetic contexts. Furthermore, the parallels between human and non-human attachment systems have prompted interdisciplinary collaborations between evolutionary psychologists, anthropologists, ethologists, and neuroscientists to unravel the underlying mechanisms and functional significance of attachment in both human and non-human animals. By scrutinizing the behavioral, physiological, and neural correlates of attachment across species, researchers have elucidated fundamental principles governing the development, maintenance, and adaptive value of attachment bonds.

5. Ancestral Environment and Human Attachment Patterns:

The concept of human attachment patterns is intrinsically linked to our ancestral environment and the historical factors that shaped our evolutionary trajectory. Our ancestors lived in small hunter-gatherer bands, where cooperation, mutual support, and shared caregiving were essential for survival. These social dynamics fostered the emergence of attachment behaviors geared towards forming and maintaining close, secure relationships. The ancestral environment, characterized by the need for collaboration and protection from external threats, likely influenced the evolution of attachment patterns centered around proximity maintenance, safe haven seeking, and secure base utilization. This adaptive response to the ancestral environment laid the groundwork for the formation of enduring social bonds and emotional connections that continue to shape human relationships today. Furthermore, the interplay between ancestral environmental pressures and genetic predispositions underscores the relationship between nature and nurture in shaping human attachment patterns. While our genetic makeup provides a foundational basis for attachment behaviors, the environmental context in which these behaviors unfold profoundly influences their manifestation and expression. Cultural variations in attachment practices also reflect the diverse ways in which ancestral environmental legacies have intersected with societal norms and values.

6. The Genetic Basis of Attachment Behaviors:

Attachment behaviors, fundamental to human social and emotional development, are deeply rooted in the genetic makeup of individuals. Understanding the genetic basis of attachment behaviors requires a multidisciplinary approach that encompasses genetics, neuroscience, and psychology. Recent research has shed light on the interplay between genetic factors and the expression of attachment behaviors. Key findings point to the role of specific genes in influencing aspects of attachment, such as the regulation of emotions, social bonding, and responses to stress. The study of monozygotic and dizygotic twins has provided compelling evidence for the heritability of attachment styles, with genetic factors explaining a significant proportion of individual differences in attachment-related characteristics. Furthermore, advances in molecular genetics have identified candidate genes implicated in the development of attachment-related behaviors, offering valuable insights into the biological mechanisms underpinning attachment. These genes are involved in a range of processes, including the synthesis and regulation of neurotransmitters such as oxytocin and vasopressin, which play pivotal roles in social bonding and affiliation. Additionally, variations in the serotonin transporter gene have been linked to differences in attachment security and vulnerability to anxiety. The influence of genetic factors on attachment extends beyond the individual level, shaping familial patterns of attachment and influencing the transmission of attachment styles across generations. Moreover, emerging evidence suggests that epigenetic mechanisms, whereby environmental factors modify gene expression, contribute to the development of attachment behaviors. This dynamic interplay between genetic predispositions and environmental influences underscores the complex nature of attachment and emphasizes the need for a holistic understanding that integrates genetic, neurobiological, and psychological perspectives.

7. Neurological Pathways and the Brain's Role in Attachment:

The exploration of neurological pathways associated with attachment behaviors has unveiled fascinating insights into the brain's multifaceted role in shaping human connections. At the heart of these revelations is the involvement of several key brain regions, particularly the amygdala, prefrontal cortex, and the hypothalamus. The amygdala, known for its pivotal role in emotional processing, is central to the evaluation of potential threats and the regulation of fear responses, crucial elements in the formation of secure attachments. Furthermore, the prefrontal cortex, responsible for higher-order cognitive functions such as decision-making and social cognition, plays an essential role in interpreting social cues, understanding others' emotions, and forming meaningful relationships. Notably, the prefrontal cortex also regulates emotional responses initiated by the amygdala, contributing to emotional regulation within attachment contexts.

In addition to these structures, the hypothalamus, a key player in regulating bodily functions and behaviors essential for survival, coordinates physiological responses linked to attachment. For instance, it governs the release of oxytocin and vasopressin, hormones known for their involvement in bonding, trust, and social affiliation. The interplay between these neurobiological mechanisms not only underpins the manifestation of attachment behaviors but also sheds light on the profound evolutionary significance of forming and maintaining social bonds.

Recent advancements in neuroimaging techniques have provided valuable neurobiological evidence supporting the complex nature of attachment processes. Functional magnetic resonance imaging (fMRI) studies have revealed heightened activation in the amygdala and prefrontal cortex when individuals engage in attachment-related tasks, demonstrating the neural correlates of attachment experiences. These findings underscore the integrated functioning of multiple brain regions in orchestrating attachment-related thoughts, feelings, and behaviors, emphasizing the deeply rooted neural foundations of human attachment.

Investigations into the impact of early caregiving experiences on neurobiological development have emphasized the critical period of neuroplasticity during which the brain undergoes significant changes in response to environmental inputs. Studies have shown that nurturing and responsive caregiving can contribute to the healthy development of neural circuits involved in attachment, highlighting the profound implications of early attachment experiences on brain architecture and subsequent socioemotional functioning. Conversely, adversity and neglect during early developmental stages have been linked to altered neural connectivity patterns, emphasizing the impact of early attachment disruptions on neurobiological processes.

8. Attachment, Survival, and Reproductive Success:

The ways in which individuals form and maintain social bonds have direct implications for their ability to thrive within their environment, protect themselves from threats, and ensure the continuation of their genetic lineage. Attachment systems, rooted in evolutionary history, have evolved as adaptive strategies to manage the complexities of human existence.

One of the key aspects of attachment's impact on survival and reproductive success lies in its influence on caregiving dynamics and social support systems. Throughout evolutionary history, individuals with strong attachment bonds were better positioned to receive care, protection, and resources from their caregivers and social networks, ultimately enhancing their chances of survival and successful reproduction. Moreover, secure attachments foster a sense of safety and emotional stability, enabling individuals to allocate more energy towards pursuits such as acquiring food, seeking shelter, and forming alliances that further contribute to their survival and reproductive fitness.

Attachment patterns have been closely linked to mating strategies and parental investment, both of which are critical components of reproductive success. Securely attached individuals often exhibit enhanced abilities to form and maintain intimate partnerships, leading to increased opportunities for successful reproduction and the upbringing of offspring in supportive environments. In contrast, insecure attachment patterns may lead to difficulties in forming stable relationships or effectively co-parenting, potentially impacting the overall reproductive success of individuals.

It is important to recognize that the interplay between attachment, survival, and reproductive success is not solely constrained to individual-level dynamics but also extends to broader societal and cultural contexts. Cultural variations in attachment practices and caregiving norms can significantly shape the adaptive value of different attachment patterns within specific social environments, thus influencing the transmission of attachment-related traits across generations. Additionally, societal structures and kinship systems can either facilitate or hinder the collective well-being and reproductive success of individuals based on the prevailing attachment dynamics within a given culture.

9. Cultural Variations and Universality in Attachment Systems:

The study of attachment has often raised the question of whether attachment systems and behaviors are culturally universal or if they vary across different societies. Understanding the interplay between culture and attachment is essential for comprehending the diverse ways in which caregivers and infants engage in attachment relationships worldwide. While attachment theory originated within Western contexts, research has increasingly focused on examining attachment dynamics in non-Western cultures to ascertain the universality of attachment patterns and explore potential cultural variations.

Cross-cultural studies have revealed both commonalities and divergences in attachment behaviors and caregiving practices across various societies. Some researchers have proposed that fundamental attachment behaviors, such as seeking proximity to caregivers in times of distress, may be universal due to their adaptive significance in ensuring survival and protection. These core attachment mechanisms, including secure base and safe haven functions, are found to exist across cultures, emphasizing their importance in human development.

However, cultural variations have also been identified, indicating that specific manifestations of attachment behaviors and parental caregiving practices can differ significantly among different cultural groups. These differences may be influenced by cultural norms, societal structures, and historical traditions, shaping familial and social dynamics that impact attachment relationships. For instance, the balance between autonomy and connectedness may vary between individualistic and collectivistic cultures, affecting the way attachment bonds are formed and maintained.

Further exploration of cultural variations in attachment systems has uncovered valuable insights into the role of socio-cultural contexts in shaping attachment styles and behaviors. Studies have highlighted the influence of cultural values, child-rearing practices, and broader family systems on the development of attachment patterns. Moreover, investigations into indigenous cultures have shed light on unique attachment dynamics that may not align with traditional Western conceptualizations, underscoring the need for a culturally sensitive approach in understanding attachment.

10. Key Studies and Experiments in Bio-Behavioral Research:

Key studies and experiments in bio-behavioral research have significantly contributed to our understanding of attachment systems and their roots in evolution. One pioneering study that has greatly influenced the field is the work of Harry Harlow, whose experiments with rhesus monkeys in the mid-20th century shed light on the significance of social contact and comfort in early development. Harlow's research demonstrated that infant monkeys preferred surrogate mothers that provided comfort over those that offered only nourishment, highlighting the critical role of emotional bonding and secure attachment in primate behavior.

In addition to Harlow's work, the Strange Situation procedure developed by Mary Ainsworth and her colleagues has become a cornerstone in attachment research. This observational study involved systematically exposing young children to a series of short separations and reunions with their caregivers in a controlled laboratory setting. The results revealed different attachment patterns, leading to the classification of infants into secure, insecure-avoidant, and insecure-ambivalent/resistant categories. This methodology has since been used worldwide to assess the quality of parent-child attachment across diverse cultures.

Further advancements in bio-behavioral research include neuroimaging studies that have illuminated the neural mechanisms underpinning attachment processes. Functional magnetic resonance imaging and electroencephalography have enabled researchers to investigate brain activity associated with attachment-related emotions and behaviors. For instance, studies have shown increased activation in brain regions such as the prefrontal cortex, amygdala, and insula during experiences of separation distress or proximity-seeking in attachment relationships.

Longitudinal studies tracking individuals from infancy to adulthood have provided crucial insights into the long-term impacts of early attachment experiences. Researchers such as Alan Sroufe and Joan Stevenson-Hinde have conducted extensive longitudinal investigations, revealing links between early attachment security and later social, emotional, and cognitive functioning. These studies have highlighted the influence of early attachment dynamics on an individual's overall well-being and interpersonal relationships.

As bio-behavioral research continues to evolve, interdisciplinary approaches integrating genetics, epigenetics, and environmental influences are shedding new light on the complex interplay of biological and relational factors in shaping attachment systems. Notably, cross-cultural studies exploring attachment norms and behaviors across diverse societies are expanding our understanding of the cultural universality and variability of attachment patterns. Through such innovative studies, we strive to deepen our comprehension of the bio-behavioral foundations of human attachment, enriching our recognition of its fundamental roles in human development and functioning.

Attachment Behaviors

1. Characteristics:

Attachment behaviors encompass a diverse array of observable actions and expressions that serve to maintain proximity, seek security, and promote emotional connectedness between individual organisms. At the core of attachment behaviors lies the fundamental drive to form and sustain close, affectionate relationships with primary caregivers or significant others. These behaviors are characterized by their adaptive nature, as they facilitate an individual's ability to manage social environments, manage stress, and foster psychological well-being. Understanding the defining characteristics of attachment behaviors is crucial for comprehending the dynamics of human relationships and the impact of early experiences on later development.

One key characteristic of attachment behaviors is the manifestation of seeking closeness and contact with attachment figures during times of distress or discomfort. This may include reaching out for physical comfort, verbal reassurance, or engaging in behaviors aimed at re-establishing proximity with a trusted caregiver. Notably, these behaviors serve as a source of emotional regulation and can offer a sense of security and protection in the face of adversity.

Additionally, attachment behaviors often involve the display of specific signals or cues that communicate one's need for support and connection. These may encompass nonverbal signals such as eye contact, facial expressions, vocalizations, or gestures that convey a desire for interaction and nurturing care. Furthermore, individuals may exhibit behaviors that signal their availability and willingness to provide care and support to their attachment figures, thus reciprocating the attachment bond.

Another defining characteristic of attachment behaviors lies in their context-specific nature, wherein the display and intensity of these behaviors are influenced by the prevailing environmental conditions. For instance, in unfamiliar or potentially threatening situations, individuals may demonstrate heightened attachment behaviors as a means of seeking protection and safety from their attachment figures. Conversely, in familiar and secure environments, these behaviors may be more subdued, allowing for exploration and autonomy while maintaining a secure base with the attachment figure.

Attachment behaviors often entail the establishment of enduring affiliative bonds, characterized by feelings of trust, emotional intimacy, and a sense of shared experiences with attachment figures. These bonds contribute to the formation of internal working models, shaping individuals' expectations of relationships and influencing their perceptions of self and others.

2. Evolutionary Perspectives on Adaptive Functions:

As we delve into the evolutionary perspectives on adaptive functions of attachment, it becomes evident that the concept of attachment behaviors has roots extending back to our early ancestors. Evolutionary theories propose that attachment serves critical adaptive functions, primarily focused on ensuring the survival and reproductive success of individuals. Viewing attachment through an evolutionary lens provides valuable insights into the biological and psychological mechanisms that underpin human behavior.

One fundamental aspect of evolutionary perspectives on attachment is the concept of kin selection and inclusive fitness. From an evolutionary standpoint, attachment behaviors can be seen as strategies to promote the survival and well-being of genetic relatives, thereby indirectly preserving and propagating shared genes. This perspective offers a compelling explanation for the strong bonds observed within family units and the inclination to protect and support kin members in times of need.

Evolutionary psychologists have highlighted the role of attachment in mediating stress and enhancing the capacity for coping with environmental challenges. Through secure attachment relationships, individuals may derive a sense of safety and predictability in their social environments, thereby reducing the physiological and psychological impacts of stressors. These adaptive functions are crucial for promoting resilience and facilitating effective responses to adversity.

In addition, evolutionary perspectives emphasize the significance of attachment in the context of reproductive success. By fostering social bonds and cooperative alliances, attachment behaviors contribute to the formation of stable mating partnerships and parental investment in offspring. The ability to form enduring attachments and manage complex social interactions enhances an individual's prospects for successful reproduction and the transmission of genetic material to future generations.

From an evolutionary viewpoint, attachment behaviors are intertwined with the development of cognitive and emotional regulatory processes. The capacity to form and maintain secure attachments supports the calibration of emotional responses and the cultivation of social cognition, both of which play pivotal roles in operating within social hierarchies and forming alliances that confer advantages in terms of resource acquisition and mate choice.

3. Attachment and Survival - Biological Imperatives:

The concept of attachment in the context of survival can be traced back to our evolutionary history, where the need for proximity to a caregiver was essential for the survival of offspring. From an evolutionary perspective, the development of attachment behaviors can be understood as a crucial adaptation that facilitated the protection, nourishment, and care of vulnerable offspring. The biological imperatives driving attachment behaviors are deeply rooted in the fundamental need for safety and security, which are pivotal for survival and thriving in any given environment.

In the early stages of human evolution, offspring who were able to maintain close proximity to their caregivers were better positioned to receive the necessary sustenance, protection from predators, and warmth essential for their survival. As a result, attachment behaviors such as proximity seeking, signaling distress, and seeking comfort from a primary caregiver became ingrained in our biological makeup as adaptive strategies for ensuring survival. These behaviors allowed for the establishment of a secure base from which individuals could explore their surroundings, engage with others, and ultimately increase their chances of reproductive success.

The role of attachment in regulating stress responses underscores its significance as a biological imperative. Secure attachment relationships have been found to mitigate the negative impact of stress, promoting emotional regulation and resilience. In contrast, insecure attachments may compromise an individual's ability to effectively manage stressors, potentially compromising their overall well-being and survival. This highlights the critical role of attachment in shaping the physiological and psychological mechanisms involved in coping with environmental challenges.

In contemporary society, the implications of attachment as a biological imperative continue to be relevant. The quality of early attachment experiences plays a vital role in shaping individuals' capacity to form and maintain healthy relationships, manage social interactions, and cope with adversities throughout the lifespan. Understanding attachment as a biological imperative provides insight into the profound influence of early caregiving experiences on an individual's developmental trajectory, mental health, and overall well-being.

4. Patterns of Attachment:

Attachment theory emphasizes the significance of early attachment relationships in shaping an individual's psychological development. One crucial aspect of this theory is the classification and interpretation of patterns of attachment that individuals may exhibit in their relationships. Ainsworth's pioneering research on the Strange Situation procedure led to the identification of three primary attachment styles: secure attachment, insecure-avoidant attachment, and insecure-ambivalent/resistant attachment.

Secure attachment, characterized by a balance between exploration and seeking proximity to the caregiver when distressed, is widely regarded as the most adaptive attachment pattern. Children with secure attachment tend to display confidence in the availability and responsiveness of their caregivers, leading to positive outcomes in social and emotional development. In contrast, children with insecure-avoidant attachment often demonstrate avoidant behaviors and minimal distress upon separation from their caregivers, reflecting a suppression of their attachment needs. On the other hand, children with insecure-ambivalent/resistant attachment exhibit clingy and anxious behaviors, along with difficulty in effectively utilizing the caregiver as a secure base for exploration.

These attachment patterns are not confined to childhood; they continue to influence individuals throughout their lives, impacting their romantic relationships, friendships, and interactions in various social contexts. The Adult Attachment Interview (AAI), developed by Mary Main and Erik Hesse, provides valuable insight into the ways in which early attachment experiences manifest in adult relationships. The AAI categorizes adults into autonomous, dismissing, preoccupied, and unresolved attachment states, shedding light on the continuity of attachment patterns across the lifespan.

Recent research has highlighted the need for cultural sensitivity and awareness when interpreting attachment patterns. Cross-cultural studies have revealed variations in attachment behaviors and interpretations, emphasizing the influence of sociocultural factors on the manifestation and understanding of attachment styles. For instance, collectivistic cultures may prioritize interdependence and communal values, influencing the expression of attachment behaviors in interpersonal relationships.

5. Proximity Seeking and Its Psychological Interpretations:

Proximity seeking is a fundamental attachment behavior observed in human infants and continues to influence social interactions throughout the lifespan. This behavior encompasses the deliberate efforts made by an individual to maintain physical closeness or contact with a significant attachment figure, typically a caregiver or a close companion. From a psychological perspective, the act of seeking proximity serves various adaptive functions that contribute to emotional regulation, sense of security, and social development.

One psychological interpretation of proximity seeking pertains to its role in establishing a secure base from which individuals can explore their environment and engage in new experiences. By seeking physical closeness to attachment figures, individuals establish a sense of safety that allows them to venture into unfamiliar territory, knowing that they have a secure base to return to in times of distress or apprehension. This interpretation aligns with attachment theory's emphasis on the dual nature of attachment behaviors, demonstrating both the striving for proximity and the concurrent pursuit of autonomy and exploration.

Proximity seeking is intertwined with the development of trust and emotional security. When individuals consistently experience responsive and comforting reactions from their attachment figures in response to their proximity seeking behaviors, they develop a sense of predictability and trust in the availability of support. This, in turn, nurtures a foundation of emotional security that fosters resilience and healthy socio-emotional development. Conversely, disruptions in proximity seeking responses, such as inconsistent or neglectful caregiving, can instigate heightened anxiety and hinder the formation of secure internal working models.

In the context of interpersonal relationships, proximity seeking plays a pivotal role in the establishment and maintenance of social bonds. Through seeking and maintaining closeness with others, individuals communicate their need for connection and intimacy, fostering reciprocal expressions of care and support. The fulfillment of these needs contributes to the development of strong, enduring relationships characterized by mutual trust and emotional attunement. Moreover, understanding the nuances of proximity seeking in relation to individual differences and cultural influences provides valuable insights into the diversities of attachment orientations and relationship dynamics across various populations.

6. Attachment in the Context of Developmental Milestones:

Attachment behaviors significantly influence the emotional and social growth of individuals from infancy through adulthood. During infancy, the development of attachment is closely linked to the achievement of key developmental milestones such as the formation of a secure base, emotional regulation, and the ability to explore the environment. Infants rely on their caregivers for comfort and support, and the quality of these early attachment relationships can shape the infant's future social and emotional development. As children transition into the toddler years, their attachment behaviors become more pronounced as they manage the challenges of gaining independence while still seeking the security of their primary caregivers. This stage often marks the emergence of separation anxiety and the increasing need for a dependable attachment figure to provide a safe haven amidst new experiences. The quality of attachment formed during these early years sets the stage for how individuals approach relationships and regulate stress throughout their lives.

In childhood, the nature of attachment continues to impact developmental milestones, as children expand their social networks beyond their immediate family. The ability to form friendships, regulate emotions, and develop empathy is influenced by the attachment relationships established in early life. Furthermore, the experience of secure attachment can foster resilience and contribute to adaptive coping strategies when faced with adversity or significant life changes. As adolescents undergo physical, cognitive, and emotional maturation, their attachment behaviors extend beyond the family unit to include romantic relationships and peer connections. The teenage years serve as a critical period for exploring the dynamics of intimate relationships, and the security established through earlier attachment figures can impact the capacity for intimacy, trust, and communication in these new contexts.

Moving into adulthood, the impact of attachment on developmental milestones continues to be profound. Forming committed partnerships, pursuing career aspirations, and transitioning to parenthood all involve the interplay between one's attachment history and current experiences. Attachment-related patterns of behavior and emotion regulation can either facilitate or hinder individuals in achieving personal and professional milestones, highlighting the significance of early attachment experiences.

7. The Role of Culture in Shaping Attachment Expressions:

From infancy to adulthood, cultural norms, practices, and beliefs significantly impact the manifestation and interpretation of attachment behaviors. In diverse cultural settings, caregivers and children engage in unique interaction patterns that reflect cultural values and priorities. The varying emphasis on independence versus interdependence, emotional expressiveness, and caregiving practices all contribute to the culturally specific manifestations of attachment behaviors. For example, in collectivist cultures, where communal values are upheld, attachment behaviors may emphasize the importance of maintaining harmony within the social group, leading to different expressions of proximity seeking and secure base behavior. Conversely, in individualistic cultures, an emphasis on autonomy and self-reliance may influence the way attachment needs are expressed and fulfilled.

Cultural narratives and traditions also play a significant role in shaping attachment orientations. Stories, rituals, and societal expectations convey implicit messages about attachment, influencing individuals' internal working models and relational patterns. These cultural influences can impact the formation of internalized schemas regarding attachment figures, separation and reunion experiences, and affect regulation strategies.

The study of cross-cultural attachment has revealed the existence of culturally distinct attachment patterns, challenging the universality of attachment theory while highlighting the dynamic interplay between culture and attachment. Researchers have identified variations in attachment security across cultural contexts, underscoring the need to consider cultural diversity in understanding attachment dynamics.

Additionally, the role of acculturation further complicates the interface between culture and attachment. Individuals adapting to multiple cultural frameworks may exhibit hybrid forms of attachment expressions, blending elements from diverse cultural backgrounds. This process of cultural integration shapes the negotiation of attachment needs and behaviors in nuanced ways, requiring a contextualized approach in studying attachment in diverse cultural contexts.

8. Individual Differences and Variability in Attachment Behaviors:

Individual differences and variability in attachment behaviors encompass a wide spectrum of emotional, behavioral, and cognitive variations that are influenced by various biological, psychological, and environmental factors. One fundamental aspect of these differences revolves around the concept of attachment styles. Research in developmental psychology has elucidated four primary attachment styles: secure, anxious-ambivalent, avoidant, and disorganized. Each style manifests distinct characteristics in interpersonal relationships, emotional regulation, and responses to stress, influencing an individual's relational patterns and coping strategies.

Individual variations in attachment behaviors can also be attributed to genetic predispositions, temperamental traits, and early caregiving experiences. Genetic studies have suggested that certain genes may influence an individual's susceptibility to developing specific attachment patterns, while temperamental traits such as adaptability, sensitivity, and reactivity contribute to the manifestation of attachment-related behaviors. Additionally, the quality of early caregiving, including parental sensitivity, consistency, and responsiveness, significantly shapes an individual's attachment orientation and social-emotional development.

Cultural contexts play a crucial role in shaping the diversity of attachment behaviors. Different cultures exhibit unique norms, beliefs, and child-rearing practices that influence the expression of attachment-related behaviors. For instance, collectivistic cultures may emphasize interdependence and closeness within family units, impacting the prevalence of certain attachment styles compared to individualistic cultures that prioritize autonomy and self-reliance.

The influence of individual differences in attachment behaviors extends beyond infancy and childhood, persisting into adulthood and impacting various aspects of relational dynamics and mental health outcomes. Understanding these individual variabilities is essential in tailoring interventions, therapeutic approaches, and support systems to address diverse attachment needs effectively.

Internal Working Models - Cognitive Schemas and Their Impact

1. Origins and Development of Cognitive Schemas

Internal working models (IWMs), first elucidated by John Bowlby, who proposed that children form mental representations of their attachment figures based on their caregiving experiences, represent a key theoretical concept within the framework of attachment theory. These cognitive schemas, developed early in life, are shaped by an individual's interactions with primary caregivers and subsequently influence their perceptions, expectations, and behaviors in relationships.

The development of cognitive schemas can be traced back to infancy, where fundamental perceptions of self, others, and the world begin to form. As children explore their environment, they gather information from their experiences and relationships, constructing mental frameworks that shape their understanding of the world. These early cognitive templates are influenced by a myriad of factors, including parental responsiveness, emotional attunement, and environmental cues. Caregiver-infant interactions play a crucial role in shaping these cognitive templates as infants learn to interpret and anticipate the responses of their primary attachment figures.

As children grow and engage with the world, their cognitive schemas continue to evolve based on ongoing experiences and relationships. Interactions with peers, educators, and other significant figures contribute to the refinement and elaboration of these internal representations. Cognitive schemas are not static; they adapt and expand as individuals encounter novel situations, acquire new knowledge, and integrate diverse perspectives.

The development of cognitive schemas is deeply intertwined with neurological and psychological processes. Neuroplasticity, the brain's ability to reorganize itself in response to experiences, plays a critical role in the formation and modification of cognitive frameworks. Moreover, cognitive developmental theories emphasize the role of social experiences and cultural contexts in shaping cognitive structures. From Piaget's stages of cognitive development to Vygotsky's sociocultural theory, scholars have highlighted the profound impact of social interactions on the construction of mental representations.

2. Theoretical Underpinnings:

Schema theory serves as the foundational framework for understanding the cognitive structures that underlie human behavior and perception. At its core, schema theory posits that individuals develop mental representations or schemas based on their experiences, which subsequently guide their processing of new information and interactions with the world. Central to this theoretical perspective is the notion that these schemas are not only formed through direct experiences but also through interpretations and internalizations of social dynamics, including early attachment relationships.

A key tenet of schema theory is the concept of assimilation and accommodation, as proposed by renowned developmental psychologist Jean Piaget. This process describes how individuals incorporate new information into existing schemas (assimilation) or modify their existing schemas to integrate new experiences (accommodation). When applied to the context of attachment and interpersonal relationships, these mechanisms elucidate how individuals interpret and make sense of their attachment-related experiences, shaping their beliefs about themselves, others, and the world around them.

Schema theory highlights the role of cognitive structures in organizing and processing emotional and interpersonal information. For instance, individuals with secure attachment schemas may tend to perceive social cues in a more constructive and positive light, fostering healthy and fulfilling relationships. In contrast, those with insecure or maladaptive schemas may exhibit cognitive biases that predispose them to perceive ambiguous social signals as threatening or rejecting, thereby influencing their behavioral responses and emotional regulation.

Additionally, the construct of schema congruence underscores the importance of examining the fit or alignment between an individual's internal working models and their current interpersonal experiences. Discrepancies between one's existing schemas and present interactions can engender cognitive dissonance and emotional turmoil, ultimately impacting the individual's psychological well-being and relational functioning. Furthermore, the integration of schema theory with attachment research has revealed the interplay between cognitive processes and affective experiences, shedding light on the mechanisms that underpin attachment-related behaviors and outcomes.

3. The Influence of Early Attachment Experiences:

The foundation of schema development is laid during the formative years, primarily through interactions with primary caregivers. As infants and young children traverse the world, they begin to form expectations about the availability and responsiveness of their caretakers. These early interactions serve as a template for understanding and interpreting relationships throughout life.

Research indicates that secure attachment experiences in early childhood cultivate positive internal working models characterized by trust, confidence, and a belief in one's worthiness of love and care. Children who receive consistent and sensitive caregiving develop a sense of security that fuels their exploration of the environment and fosters healthy social and emotional development. Conversely, inconsistent or neglectful caregiving can lead to the formation of insecure attachment styles, manifesting as anxious, avoidant, or disorganized behaviors.

The impact of early attachment experiences extends beyond childhood, influencing the quality of adult relationships and overall well-being. Individuals with secure attachment histories often exhibit greater resilience, empathy, and capacity for intimacy in their romantic partnerships, friendships, and familial relations. In contrast, those with insecure attachment patterns may struggle with issues related to trust, dependency, and emotional regulation, leading to challenges in forming and maintaining healthy connections.

Early attachment experiences can shape an individual's response to stress and adversity later in life. Securely attached individuals tend to display adaptive coping strategies when faced with challenges, drawing on their positive internal working models to seek support and find comfort in relationships. In contrast, individuals with insecure attachment orientations may experience heightened distress and difficulties in seeking and receiving effective support.

Understanding the influence of early attachment experiences provides valuable insights into the interconnectedness of early development, mental health, and interpersonal relationships. It underscores the significance of promoting secure attachment dynamics to lay the groundwork for resilient, emotionally attuned, and fulfilling lives. By recognizing the profound impact of these formative experiences, we can strive to create environments that nurture secure attachments and facilitate healthy schema development, ultimately contributing to individuals' long-term well-being and relational satisfaction.

4. Schema Activation and Application:

When individuals encounter situations or stimuli reminiscent of past attachment experiences, their internal schemas are activated, leading to a diverse range of emotional, cognitive, and behavioral responses. These activated schemas serve as lenses through which individuals perceive and interpret their interpersonal interactions and relationships. Central to this process is the application of these activated schemas in guiding one's responses and decisions within various relational contexts. The interplay between schema activation and application sheds light on the way individuals orchestrate their attachment-related experiences. It is important to acknowledge that schema activation can occur both consciously and unconsciously, exerting significant influence on an individual's emotional regulation, problem-solving strategies, and interpersonal dynamics. Additionally, the salience and intensity of schema activation can vary based on the nature and chronicity of early attachment experiences. Furthermore, the adaptiveness or maladaptiveness of these activated schemas greatly impacts an individual's capacity to form and maintain secure, healthy relationships. In instances where early attachment experiences have been characterized by insecurity or trauma, the activation and application of corresponding schemas may lead to relational difficulties, heightened vulnerability to distress, and defensive coping strategies. Conversely, individuals with secure attachment experiences may demonstrate more flexible and adaptive schema activation and application, fostering supportive and enriching interpersonal connections. Understanding the nuanced processes of schema activation and application provides valuable insights into the complexities of human attachment and the ways in which early experiences continue to reverberate throughout adulthood.

5. Impact on Interpersonal Relationships:

Research indicates that individuals with secure internal working models tend to develop more trusting, empathetic, and mutually supportive relationships. These individuals exhibit a capacity for effective communication, emotional regulation, and intimacy, fostering healthier and more fulfilling connections with others. In contrast, insecure or disorganized internal models may lead to difficulties in forming and maintaining close relationships, often characterized by patterns of mistrust, dependency, or avoidance.

The impact of internal working models extends beyond romantic relationships to encompass familial, platonic, and professional interactions. Individuals with secure internal models typically demonstrate resilience and adaptability in functioning within diverse social environments, building strong social support networks, and fostering positive social dynamics. Conversely, those with insecure or dysfunctional schemas may encounter challenges in establishing and maintaining meaningful connections, leading to feelings of isolation, conflict, or emotional distress.

The influence of internal working models on interpersonal relationships is evident in the transmission of attachment patterns across generations. Parents' internal models can significantly shape the attachment experiences of their children, perpetuating either secure or insecure attachment styles within family systems. The intergenerational impact underscores the significance of these cognitive schemas on the quality of close relationships within society.

Understanding the impact of internal working models on interpersonal relationships holds vital implications for clinical practice and intervention strategies. Recognizing the influence of early attachment experiences and subsequent cognitive schemas can inform therapeutic approaches aimed at promoting secure attachment and enhancing relational functioning. By addressing maladaptive cognitive schemas and fostering positive relationship dynamics, interventions can mitigate the detrimental effects of insecure attachment patterns and facilitate healthier, more fulfilling interpersonal connections.

6. Vulnerability to Dysfunctional Patterns:

Vulnerability to dysfunctional patterns within the framework of internal working models reflects the interplay between early attachment experiences and the cognitive schemas that underpin individuals' perceptions, expectations, and behaviors in relationships. These dysfunctional patterns often manifest as maladaptive coping strategies, rigid interpersonal dynamics, and struggles with emotional regulation.

The roots of vulnerability to dysfunctional patterns can be traced back to the formative years when attachment bonds are initially established. Insecure or disorganized attachment experiences may give rise to negative working models of self and others, predisposing individuals to interpret interactions through a lens of mistrust, unworthiness, or unpredictability. Such distorted perceptions can prompt maladaptive responses, including heightened sensitivity to rejection, fear of intimacy, or difficulty establishing and sustaining healthy relationships.

Individuals with vulnerable internal working models may exhibit patterns of behavior characterized by oscillations between excessive reliance on others for validation and independence, or a persistent avoidance of closeness and emotional expression. These patterns can perpetuate cycles of relational distress and instability, hindering the ability to form secure, fulfilling connections with others.

Vulnerability to dysfunctional patterns can significantly impact one's mental and emotional well-being, contributing to heightened stress, anxiety, and depression. The internalization of negative self-beliefs and distrust in others can create a pervasive sense of inadequacy and isolation, further exacerbating the challenges associated with forming and maintaining gratifying interpersonal relationships.

Addressing vulnerability to dysfunctional patterns necessitates a multi-faceted approach encompassing both individual and relational interventions. Cognitive-behavioral techniques aimed at identifying and challenging maladaptive schemas, as well as fostering alternative, more adaptive ways of relating, constitute core components of therapeutic endeavors. Additionally, cultivating self-awareness and mindfulness can empower individuals to recognize and regulate their emotional responses, thus minimizing the impact of dysfunctional patterns.

The exploration of past attachment experiences and their influence on current relationship dynamics is integral to promoting healing and transformation. By fostering a safe therapeutic environment that encourages exploration and processing of early attachment wounds, individuals can gradually dismantle dysfunctional schemas, replace them with healthier paradigms, and develop more secure and positive relational patterns.

7. Mechanisms for Schema Change and Adaptation:

Mechanisms for schema change and adaptation encompass a complex interplay of cognitive processes, emotional regulation, and interpersonal experiences. One prominent mechanism involves cognitive restructuring, wherein individuals challenge and modify their existing schemas through reflective introspection and external feedback. This process allows for the incorporation of new information and experiences, leading to an evolution of one's internal working model.

Adaptive coping strategies play a pivotal role in facilitating schema change. Individuals may engage in cognitive reappraisal, where they reinterpret their past attachment experiences in a more constructive light, thereby fostering resilience and promoting a positive restructuring of their internal working models. Additionally, the cultivation of secure positive relationships can bring about a profound shift in one's internal models, providing a corrective emotional experience that challenges previously held maladaptive beliefs and perceptions.

Another essential mechanism for schema change lies in the sphere of psychological interventions. Therapeutic approaches such as cognitive-behavioral therapy (CBT) and attachment-based interventions offer individuals the opportunity to explore, understand, and modify their internal working models through a collaborative and supportive therapeutic relationship. By addressing cognitive distortions and bolstering emotional regulation, these interventions empower individuals to actively adapt their schema patterns towards healthier, more secure representations.

On the other hand, neurobiological research has shed light on the connection between neural plasticity and schema adaptation. Studies have demonstrated the brain's remarkable capacity for reorganization and adaptation, providing a biological foundation for the malleability of internal working models. Understanding the neural underpinnings of schema change offers valuable insights into the potential for targeted interventions aimed at promoting adaptive transformations within individuals' attachment systems.

Importantly, the dynamic nature of schema change necessitates a holistic approach that encompasses both individual efforts and environmental influences. Collaborative efforts between individuals, caregivers, and mental health professionals can create a conducive environment for fostering adaptive schema alterations, ultimately enhancing overall well-being and relational functioning. Recognizing the multifaceted nature of mechanisms for schema change and adaptation underscores the importance of comprehensive interventions that address cognitive, emotional, and relational dimensions, thereby fostering optimal growth and development.

8. Longitudinal Perspectives on Schema Stability:

Longitudinal studies focusing on the stability of internal working models have been instrumental in expanding our understanding of attachment and its long-term implications. These comprehensive investigations track individuals over extended periods, providing valuable insights into the persistence and evolution of cognitive schemas related to attachment. One of the fundamental findings across longitudinal research is the relative stability of internal working models over time, particularly in the absence of significant life events or interventions aimed at restructuring these schemas. This stability underscores the impact of early attachment experiences on individuals' psychological framework for relating to others.

Longitudinal studies have highlighted that while there is a general tendency for internal working models to exhibit stability, they are not entirely immutable. Certain life transitions, such as forming new intimate relationships, becoming a parent, or experiencing loss, can serve as catalysts for reevaluating and reshaping existing cognitive schemas. These pivotal moments provide opportunities for individuals to revisit their attachment orientations and adapt them to meet the demands of evolving interpersonal contexts.

Examining the trajectories of schema stability across different developmental stages has also yielded critical insights. For instance, longitudinal research has demonstrated that adolescents and young adults may demonstrate more fluctuation in their internal working models compared to older adults, suggesting that these schemas are subject to dynamic shifts during formative life stages. This nuanced understanding brings attention to the importance of considering contextual influences and developmental tasks when evaluating the stability of attachment-related cognitive schemas.

Longitudinal perspectives on schema stability have shed light on the interplay between individual differences and environmental factors in shaping attachment representations over time. By following individuals from childhood to adulthood, researchers have discerned how diverse experiences, such as trauma, support, or chronic stress, interact with inherent personality traits to either bolster or challenge the stability of internal working models. This holistic approach fosters a richer comprehension of the multifaceted nature of attachment and elucidates the complex pathways through which schema stability unfolds across the lifespan.

The Role of the Caregiver - Sensitivity, Responsiveness, and Influences on Development

1. Sensitivity in the Caregiving Context:

Sensitivity in the caregiving context refers to the ability of a caregiver to be attuned and responsive to the needs and cues of the child. It involves the caregiver's ability to accurately perceive, interpret, and appropriately respond to the child's signals, emotions, and behaviors. This responsiveness is crucial for creating a secure attachment bond, as it communicates to the child that their needs are understood and will be met, fostering a sense of security and trust within the relationship. Sensitivity reflects the caregiver's capacity to provide comfort, support, and guidance in a manner that is tailored to the individual child's temperament and emotional state. This adaptability is essential for promoting healthy socioemotional development and laying the foundation for future relationships. Research has consistently demonstrated the significant impact of sensitive caregiving on a child's emotional regulation, social competence, and overall well-being. Moreover, it has been found that children who experience sensitive caregiving tend to demonstrate more positive affect, increased exploration and curiosity, and greater resilience in the face of stress or adversity. Understanding the nuances of sensitivity in caregiving involves recognizing the dynamic interplay between the caregiver and child, as well as the contextual factors that may influence the caregiver's ability to be sensitive and responsive. These factors may include parental stress, mental health, cultural beliefs, and socioeconomic status, all of which can shape the quality of caregiving interactions. Importantly, sensitivity is not synonymous with indulgence or overprotection; rather, it entails a balanced approach that respects the child's autonomy while providing the necessary support and guidance. Developing sensitivity as a caregiver requires reflection, empathy, and an openness to continually attune to the child's evolving needs and emotions.

2. Responsiveness:

Throughout early childhood, parents who consistently respond to their child's bids for attention, comfort, and connection provide a secure framework within which the child can explore the world. This secure base is pivotal in fostering a sense of safety and trust, allowing the child to venture forth knowing that they can return to a reliable source of support. Furthermore, responsive caregiving nurtures the development of strong attachment bonds, enabling children to form secure internal working models that influence their future relationships and emotional resilience.

By thoughtfully considering children's vocalizations, gestures, and expressions, responsive caregivers demonstrate validation and empathy, encouraging healthy socio-emotional development. As children grow older, responsive interactions continue to bolster their self-esteem, as they internalize a sense of being heard and understood. Moreover, consistent responsiveness helps children regulate their emotions and develop coping strategies, contributing to their overall well-being and mental health.

A developmental perspective on responsiveness also underscores its role in shaping children's social skills and adaptive behaviors. Through sensitive and responsive care, children learn how to express their needs, interpret others' intentions, and manage complex social dynamics. Additionally, being consistently met with responsiveness cultivates a sense of security, empowering children to explore and engage confidently, thereby promoting the acquisition of new skills and knowledge.

Research has demonstrated that parental responsiveness correlates with enhanced language development, as the reciprocal nature of conversational turn-taking promotes linguistic competence and comprehension. By iteratively responding to a child's verbal attempts, caregivers scaffold their language acquisition, facilitating the emergence of vocabulary, syntax, and pragmatic capabilities.

3. The Impact of Consistent vs. Inconsistent Caregiving:

When caregivers consistently provide nurturing, responsive, and attentive care, children are more likely to form secure attachments. These secure attachments serve as a foundation for healthy social and emotional development, enabling children to explore their environment with confidence and seek comfort from their caregivers when needed. In contrast, inconsistent caregiving, marked by unpredictable responses, can lead to insecurity and anxiety in children.

Studies have demonstrated that children who experience consistent caregiving tend to exhibit greater resilience and adaptability. They are better equipped to regulate their emotions, develop trusting relationships, and manage social challenges. This consistency fosters a sense of safety and predictability, allowing children to internalize a positive sense of self-worth and competence. Conversely, inconsistent caregiving can hinder the formation of secure attachments, leading to attachment insecurity and potentially impacting a child's future relationships and mental well-being.

Inconsistency in caregiving can manifest in various forms, including fluctuating levels of parental engagement, erratic responsiveness to a child's needs, and unpredictable availability. These inconsistencies can disrupt the natural progression of attachment formation, as children may struggle to understand and predict their caregivers' behaviors. As a result, they may develop hypervigilance or ambivalence in relationships, exhibiting patterns of insecure attachment characterized by anxiety, avoidance, or disorganization.

Inconsistent caregiving has been linked to adverse outcomes, such as heightened stress reactivity, impaired self-regulation, and difficulties in establishing trust and intimacy. Children raised in environments with inconsistent caregiving may encounter challenges in forming healthy peer relationships, managing stress, and regulating their emotions effectively. These repercussions can extend into adulthood, potentially impacting romantic relationships, parenting practices, and overall psychological well-being.

4. Patterns of Attachment - Secure, Avoidant, Ambivalent, and Disorganized:

In the field of attachment theory, researchers have identified distinct patterns of attachment that emerge in the relationships between children and their caregivers. These patterns, established during early childhood, greatly influence an individual's socio-emotional development and their ability to form and maintain relationships throughout their lifespan. The four primary attachment patterns are secure, avoidant, ambivalent, and disorganized.

Secure attachment is characterized by a child's use of the caregiver as a secure base from which to explore the world. When the caregiver is present, the child feels safe and able to engage with the environment, but they may display distress when separated. Securely attached children seek comfort and support from their caregivers when distressed, and readily accept it when offered.

Conversely, avoidant attachment is marked by the child's apparent self-sufficiency and minimal seeking of proximity to the caregiver. These children may actively avoid or ignore the caregiver upon reunion after a period of separation, displaying little overt signs of distress. This behavior reflects a learned expectation that their needs for comfort and reassurance will not be met.

Ambivalent attachment is characterized by an inconsistent response to the caregiver's availability. Children with this attachment pattern may display heightened distress upon separation, yet demonstrate ambivalence or resistance when the caregiver attempts to provide comfort upon reunion. This reflects their uncertainty about the caregiver's availability and responsiveness.

The disorganized attachment pattern is marked by conflicting behaviors, such as seeking and avoiding proximity simultaneously or showing disoriented, dazed, or apprehensive behavior in the presence of the caregiver. This pattern often emerges in the context of severe neglect, abuse, or other forms of parental behavior that instills fear in the child.

Understanding these attachment patterns is crucial for professionals working with children and families, as they provide insights into the dynamics of the caregiver-child relationship and can inform interventions aimed at fostering healthy attachment bonds. Moreover, recognizing and respecting the diversity of attachment patterns across cultures is essential to providing culturally sensitive support to children and families from varied backgrounds.

5. Cultural Variations in Caregiving Practices and Their Implications:

Every culture has its unique values, belief systems, and social norms that inform the approach to child-rearing, influencing the ways in which caregivers interact with and nurture their children. These cultural variations in caregiving practices encompass a broad spectrum, from the emphasis on independence and self-reliance in individualistic cultures to the collectivist ethos prioritizing interdependence and harmony in communal societies.

In individualistic cultures, such as those prevalent in Western societies, parenting practices often lean towards fostering autonomy and self-expression in children. Encouraging independence and assertiveness is considered essential for personal growth and success. In contrast, collectivist cultures, typically observed in many Asian, African, and Latin American societies, place a strong emphasis on group cohesion and familial interconnectedness. Consequently, caregiving behaviors in these cultures often prioritize nurturing relationships, empathy, and cooperation, with an emphasis on preserving social harmony.

Cultural perspectives also influence the degree of emphasis placed on specific parenting dimensions, such as warmth, control, discipline, and educational expectations. For instance, some cultures may prioritize strict discipline and academic achievement as indicators of good parenting, while others may value emotional closeness and support as central tenets of effective caregiving. These cultural variations significantly shape the development of internal working models in children, influencing their beliefs about themselves, others, and relationships.

The implications of cultural variations in caregiving practices extend beyond the immediate family unit, impacting broader social structures and community dynamics. Understanding these cultural influences is crucial for professionals working with diverse populations, including educators, mental health practitioners, and policymakers. It is essential to recognize and respect the diversity of caregiving practices while providing support and interventions that are sensitive to cultural nuances and context. By acknowledging and embracing cultural diversity in caregiving, practitioners can foster inclusive and equitable approaches to promoting secure attachments and healthy child development across varying cultural contexts.

6. Parental Stress and Its Effect on Parenting Styles:

Parental stress can significantly impact parenting styles and, subsequently, the quality of caregiving children receive. When parents experience high levels of stress, they may struggle to exhibit the patience, consistency, and responsiveness required for nurturing secure attachments with their children. The effects of parental stress on parenting styles can manifest in various ways, such as decreased emotional availability, compromised communication, and diminished ability to provide a stable and nurturing environment. Consequently, these challenges can lead to disruptions in the development of secure attachment patterns in children. Understanding the relationship between parental stress and parenting styles is critical for creating effective interventions and support systems for families. Research has consistently shown that high levels of stress can lead to increased authoritarian or neglectful parenting styles, both of which have been associated with negative outcomes for children. Authoritarian parenting, characterized by strict rules and discipline without warmth or responsiveness, can contribute to feelings of insecurity and low self-esteem in children. Additionally, neglectful parenting, resulting from the overwhelming demands of stress, can create an environment lacking in emotional support and consistent care, potentially leading to attachment-related difficulties. It is essential to address parental stress and its implications through targeted interventions, including stress management techniques, social support networks, and mental health services. By equipping parents with the resources to manage stress effectively, the aim is to mitigate its potential impact on parenting styles and, ultimately, promote healthier family dynamics and secure attachments. Recognizing the complex interplay between parental stress and parenting styles also underscores the importance of holistic approaches to supporting families, which address not only the individual well-being of parents but also the broader family context.

7. Longitudinal Studies - Correlations Between Early Caregiving and Later Life Outcomes:

Longitudinal studies on the correlations between early caregiving and later life outcomes have shed light on the profound impact that the quality of caregiver interactions can have on an individual's long-term development. These extensive research endeavors have followed individuals from infancy into adulthood, meticulously documenting the nature of their early attachment experiences and subsequently tracing the trajectory of their psychological, emotional, and social well-being. The findings from these longitudinal studies have consistently underscored the critical significance of early caregiving in shaping lifelong cognitive and emotional functioning. The evidence reveals that children who experienced sensitive and responsive caregiving tend to exhibit greater resilience and adaptive capacity well into their adult years. Furthermore, these individuals often demonstrate higher levels of socioemotional competence, forming more secure and trusting relationships with others. Conversely, individuals who experienced inconsistent or neglectful caregiving in their formative years may display heightened vulnerability to mental health challenges, including anxiety, depression, and relational difficulties. By elucidating these complex linkages between early caregiving and later life outcomes, longitudinal studies have unveiled the influence that parental behaviors wield on offspring's psychological adjustment and overall well-being. Moreover, this body of research serves as a compelling impetus for developing targeted interventions aimed at bolstering parental capacities and ameliorating the intergenerational transmission of negative caregiving patterns. As we delve deeper into the nuanced findings of these longitudinal studies, it becomes unequivocally evident that the impact of early caregiving reverberates across the lifespan, significantly influencing an individual's propensity for resilience, mental health, and socialization. The implications of this research extend far beyond academia, permeating clinical practice, public policy, and societal discourse, compelling us to reevaluate the foundational importance of nurturing, empathetic caregiving in fostering thriving, well-adjusted individuals within our communities.

8. Interventions and Support Systems for Enhancing Parental Skills:

Parenting interventions and support systems play a crucial role in enhancing parental skills, promoting healthy child development, and fostering secure attachment relationships. These programs encompass a wide range of strategies aimed at equipping caregivers with the knowledge, resources, and support necessary to optimize their caregiving practices. One prominent approach involves the provision of educational workshops and training sessions that focus on areas such as positive discipline techniques, effective communication, and understanding children's emotional needs. By empowering parents with evidence-based insights and practical tools, these interventions aim to bolster parental confidence and competence, ultimately leading to more nurturing and responsive caregiving. Additionally, family therapy and counseling services offer a valuable platform for addressing interpersonal dynamics, resolving conflicts, and strengthening the parent-child bond. Through guided discussions and therapeutic interventions, caregivers are able to explore their own attachment histories, develop insight into their parenting styles, and cultivate healthier relational patterns within the family unit. Furthermore, community-based initiatives, such as parent support groups and early childhood development programs, provide a vital network of peer support, guidance, and collaborative learning opportunities. These environments create a sense of belonging and solidarity among caregivers, offering avenues for sharing experiences, seeking advice, and accessing community resources. In parallel, outreach efforts by healthcare professionals, social workers, and child development specialists contribute to identifying at-risk families, delivering targeted interventions, and connecting caregivers with essential services. The utilization of home visiting programs can afford personalized support, developmental assessments, and tailored interventions within the familiar context of the family home. Moreover, the integration of technology-based tools, such as mobile applications and online resources, offers convenient access to information, interactive parenting guides, and virtual communities, further extending the reach of parental support services. Finally, policy advocacy and investment in early childhood education initiatives serve to create systemic changes that recognize the critical role of caregivers in shaping the developmental trajectory of children. By prioritizing resources for parental support and education, societies can promote a culture of parenting that values sensitivity, responsiveness, and the holistic well-being of children.

The Dynamics of the Attachment System - Mechanisms of Activation and Deactivation

1. Attachment Triggers - The Role of Environmental and Internal Cues:

The attachment system, deeply rooted in evolutionary history, is a complex, adaptive mechanism that governs human social behavior and emotional regulation. Understanding the triggers that activate or deactivate this system is crucial to comprehending human relationships and psychological well-being. Environmental cues encompass a broad range of stimuli, including social interactions, physical proximity, and relational dynamics. These cues can emanate from primary caregivers, peers, romantic partners, or even strangers, playing a pivotal role in shaping individuals' attachment patterns. Furthermore, contextual factors such as cultural norms and societal expectations contribute to the interpretation and salience of these triggers, thereby influencing attachment-related behaviors. Internal cues, on the other hand, pertain to the individual's own cognitive, emotional, and physiological responses to attachment-relevant stimuli. These may include memories of past relational experiences, self-perceptions, and affective states, all of which can profoundly impact the activation or deactivation of the attachment system. It is essential to recognize that the interplay between external and internal cues is not only complex but also subject to dynamic variations across developmental stages and relational contexts. Moreover, advancements in neurobiological research have shed light on the neural mechanisms underlying the processing of attachment cues. Neuroimaging studies have revealed the involvement of brain regions such as the amygdala, prefrontal cortex, and insula in detecting and responding to attachment-related signals, highlighting the interplay between biological processes and attachment dynamics. These findings emphasize the interconnectedness of psychological and physiological components in the orchestration of attachment triggers.

2. Neurobiological Underpinnings of the Attachment System:

The neurobiological underpinnings of the attachment system provide a fascinating insight into the mechanisms that govern human connection and bonding. At the core of these underpinnings is the concept of neurotransmitters, hormones, and brain structures that play pivotal roles in shaping attachment behaviors and responses. One of the key neurotransmitters involved in attachment is oxytocin, often referred to as the 'love hormone' or 'bonding hormone'. Oxytocin is released in response to social cues such as touch, eye contact, and nurturing interactions, promoting feelings of trust, empathy, and closeness. Studies have shown that increased levels of oxytocin are associated with enhanced social bonding and affiliative behaviors, highlighting its significance in the attachment process. Additionally, the role of dopamine, a neurotransmitter linked to pleasure and reward, has been implicated in reinforcing attachment-related behaviors. The activation of the brain's reward pathways in response to interactions with attachment figures further reinforces the significance of neurobiological components in fostering and maintaining close relationships. Importantly, the brain structures involved in processing and regulating attachment-related information are also integral to understanding the neurobiology of attachment. The prefrontal cortex, amygdala, and hippocampus play crucial roles in interpreting social cues, assessing threats, and encoding emotional memories, respectively. These brain regions work in harmony to facilitate the recognition of attachment triggers, the regulation of emotional responses, and the formation of internal working models that influence future relational patterns. Furthermore, the ongoing interplay between the neurobiological substrates of the attachment system and environmental stimuli underscores the dynamic nature of attachment processes. Environmental experiences and caregiving dynamics can shape the development and functioning of the neural circuits involved in attachment, contributing to individual differences in attachment styles and adaptive strategies. This dynamic interplay between biology and environment highlights the complex and nuanced nature of the attachment system, emphasizing the need for a holistic understanding that incorporates both neurobiological and psychosocial dimensions.

3. The Process of Activation:

When individuals encounter situations or stimuli that signal potential harm or danger, the attachment system is engaged to prompt protective actions and seek proximity to a secure figure. This process involves a complex interplay of cognitive, emotional, and behavioral mechanisms that have been shaped by evolutionary forces and early caregiving experiences.

At its core, activation involves the recognition and interpretation of cues that signify potential threats to one's well-being. These cues can be both external, such as sudden loud noises or looming physical danger, and internal, including feelings of anxiety, uncertainty, or distress. The brain's neural circuitry orchestrates the rapid assessment and processing of these cues, often leading to heightened vigilance and readiness for action. Moreover, past experiences and memories stored in internal working models influence how individuals perceive and respond to these triggers, highlighting the significant impact of early attachment relationships on subsequent functioning.

Once a potential threat is detected, the individual's attachment system becomes activated, triggering a cascade of physiological and psychological responses aimed at reducing the perceived risk and restoring a sense of safety. These responses can manifest as increased arousal, hypervigilance, and a heightened need for proximity to a trusted caregiver or attachment figure. Importantly, seeking proximity serves as a primary adaptive strategy to regulate emotions, receive comfort, and obtain support during times of distress, thereby promoting a re-establishment of emotional equilibrium.

The process of activation also involves the dynamic interplay between the individual's appraisal of the threat and the availability and responsiveness of the attachment figure. If the figure is perceived as accessible and supportive, the individual is more likely to seek and receive comfort, leading to a reduction in physiological arousal and an alleviation of distress. However, if the attachment figure is perceived as distant, unresponsive, or unreliable, the individual may experience prolonged states of distress and struggle to effectively downregulate their negative emotions.

The process of seeking proximity and the subsequent response from the attachment figure lay the foundation for the development and maintenance of secure or insecure attachment patterns. Consistent and sensitive caregiving fosters a secure base from which individuals can confidently explore their surroundings and manage challenges, while inconsistent or inadequate care can lead to the formation of insecure attachment styles characterized by difficulties in regulating emotional responses and managing stress.

4. Patterns of Deactivation:

Patterns of deactivation in the attachment system reflect a range of strategies utilized by individuals to mitigate distress and regulate emotions in the face of perceived threats or stressors. These deactivation patterns can manifest in various ways, including emotional distancing, cognitive disengagement, and active suppression of attachment-related thoughts and feelings. These strategies are often adaptive responses aimed at reducing anxiety and maintaining a sense of psychological equilibrium. Emotional distancing involves creating an internal emotional barrier to shield oneself from overwhelming feelings of vulnerability or dependency, resulting in a decreased reliance on others for support. Cognitive disengagement entails redirecting attention away from attachment-related concerns, allowing individuals to temporarily alleviate distress by focusing on alternative activities or thoughts. Active suppression of attachment-related thoughts and feelings involves conscious efforts to inhibit the activation of the attachment system, effectively minimizing the impact of attachment-related cues on emotional states. While these deactivation patterns can offer short-term relief from distress, they may also impede the potential for secure attachments and limit the depth of relational connections. The influence of attachment styles on deactivation strategies is notable, as individuals with avoidant attachment tendencies may exhibit more pronounced forms of deactivation, while those with anxious attachment styles might engage in cyclical patterns of activation and deactivation. Contextual factors such as past experiences, social support networks, and cultural norms further shape the utilization of deactivation strategies. Understanding these patterns is critical not only for comprehending individual differences in attachment behaviors but also for informing therapeutic interventions aimed at promoting secure and adaptive attachment dynamics.

5. Attachment Styles and Their Influence on Activation/Deactivation Dynamics:

Attachment styles, categorized as secure, anxious-preoccupied, dismissive-avoidant, and fearful-avoidant, are established during early interactions with primary caregivers and continue to influence interpersonal relationships throughout the lifespan. Understanding how these attachment styles impact activation and deactivation dynamics is crucial for comprehending an individual's behavioral responses to attachment-related situations. The secure attachment style, characterized by a positive view of self and others, tends to promote effective regulation of the attachment system. Individuals with a secure attachment style demonstrate a balanced approach to proximity seeking and exploration, allowing them to effectively manage activation and deactivation processes. Conversely, individuals with an anxious-preoccupied attachment style often exhibit hyperactivation of the attachment system, leading to heightened vigilance, exaggerated proximity seeking, and difficulties in calming themselves when distressed. This pattern of overactivation can result in challenges with deactivating the attachment system, often prolonging distress and impeding the return to a sense of safety. On the other hand, individuals with a dismissive-avoidant attachment style may adopt a strategy of deactivating the attachment system through maintaining emotional distance and self-reliance. This approach can lead to minimizing the perception of threat but may also hinder the expression of genuine needs and emotions. Furthermore, individuals with a fearful-avoidant attachment style experience a combination of both hyperactivation and deactivation, oscillating between intense proximity seeking and avoidance behaviors. Their struggle to regulate the attachment system may stem from conflicting desires for closeness and fear of rejection or harm. It is important to recognize that attachment styles are not fixed but can be influenced by subsequent experiences and relational dynamics. Interventions aimed at modifying attachment styles have shown promise in promoting more adaptive activation and deactivation patterns, fostering greater relational satisfaction and emotional well-being.

6. The Role of Anxiety and Avoidance in System Modulation:

Anxiety and avoidance are key components in the modulation of the attachment system, exerting profound influence on individuals' responses to social interactions, emotional intimacy, and relational dynamics. Within the framework of attachment theory, anxious attachment involves a heightened sensitivity to cues of potential rejection or abandonment, often resulting in hyperactivation of the attachment system. Individuals with anxious attachment tendencies may exhibit a persistent need for reassurance, intense emotional reactions to perceived threats to the relationship, and a propensity to engage in protest behaviors when feeling insecure. On the other hand, avoidance, as a contrasting attachment style, manifests as a deliberate withdrawal from intimate emotional connections and a suppression of attachment-related needs. This defensive deactivation of the attachment system serves the purpose of minimizing vulnerability and maintaining independence, but often leads to emotional distance and a reluctance to rely on others for support. Understanding the interplay between anxiety and avoidance is crucial in comprehending the modulation of the attachment system, as these two dimensions interact in complex ways to shape individuals' relational behaviors and coping strategies. Research has shown that individuals with anxious and avoidant attachment styles may experience internal conflict and ambivalence when managing interpersonal relationships, leading to an oscillation between desperate bids for closeness and defensive detachment. Furthermore, the presence of chronic stressors, unresolved traumas, or inconsistent caregiving experiences can exacerbate the manifestation of anxiety and avoidance, further complicating the modulation of the attachment system. Recognizing the impact of these attachment patterns on emotional regulation, communication, and conflict resolution is paramount in clinical and therapeutic settings, as it provides valuable insights into the underlying dynamics of relationship distress and maladaptive coping mechanisms.

7. Psychosocial Influences:

The dynamics of the attachment system are closely intertwined with psychosocial influences that encompass various stressors, sources of support, and stability factors. Stressors, whether acute or chronic, play a significant role in shaping individuals' attachment patterns and behaviors. In the face of stress, the attachment system is activated, often leading individuals to seek proximity to their attachment figures for comfort and reassurance. Moreover, the nature and intensity of stressors can impact the modulation of avoidance and anxiety within the attachment system, influencing the individual's coping strategies. Understanding the diverse array of stressors that can impact attachment dynamics is crucial in comprehending the complexities of human behavior within relationships. Equally important are the sources of support available to individuals during times of stress. Supportive relationships provide a vital buffer against the negative effects of stress on attachment processes, promoting a sense of security and trust that fosters adaptive responses to challenging situations. Whether it be the presence of a responsive caregiver in early development or the support of romantic partners and close friends in adulthood, the availability of supportive bonds bolsters individuals' capacity to manage the ebbs and flows of life with greater resilience. Furthermore, stability factors, such as consistency in caregiving, environmental predictability, and relational constancy, contribute to the establishment of secure attachment and serve as foundational pillars for emotional well-being. Variations in these stability factors can shape attachment trajectories across the lifespan, illustrating the impact of psychosocial influences on attachment dynamics. Recognizing the interplay between stressors, support, and stability factors elucidates the complexity of the attachment system and underscores the significance of considering broader contextual elements in understanding the nuances of human attachment.

8. Lifespan Perspective - Changes in Activation/Deactivation Patterns Over Time:

As individuals progress through life, the dynamics of their attachment system undergo significant transformations. From the early formative years to later stages of development and adulthood, varying experiences and environmental influences shape the activation and deactivation patterns within the attachment system. In infancy and early childhood, dependency on primary caregivers is crucial for survival, resulting in a heightened sensitivity to cues that trigger attachment behaviors. During this stage, the activation of the attachment system occurs frequently in response to perceived threats or stressors, with seeking proximity to secure figures serving as a primary coping mechanism. However, as children grow and gain more autonomy, the need for proximity maintenance may fluctuate, leading to shifts in the frequency and intensity of activation and deactivation processes. Adolescence marks a period of increased independence-seeking and exploration, which can further impact the attachment system dynamics. The balance between the desire for autonomy and the continued need for emotional support from attachment figures often shapes the activation and deactivation patterns during this transitional phase. As individuals transition into adulthood, forming intimate partnerships and establishing new caregiving roles can significantly alter the activation and deactivation mechanisms. The interplay between romantic relationships, parenting responsibilities, and career demands all contribute to the evolving dynamics of the attachment system. Furthermore, factors such as loss, trauma, and major life transitions can elicit pronounced changes in activation and deactivation patterns across the lifespan, influencing how individuals seek and utilize interpersonal connections for comfort and security. Understanding these lifespan perspectives on attachment dynamics provides valuable insights into human behavior, mental health, and interpersonal relationships.

Exploration, the Secure Base, and Autonomy

1. The Secure Base Phenomenon - Origins and Functions:

Originating from the pioneering work of John Bowlby, the notion of a secure base refers to the role of a primary caregiver or attachment figure in providing a safe and reliable foundation from which an individual can confidently explore their environment. This phenomenon is crucial not only in childhood but also in shaping adult relationships and emotional well-being. The secure base offers a haven of security and support, enabling individuals to engage in exploratory behaviors with the confidence that they have a dependable source of comfort to return to when needed.

The functions of the secure base are multifaceted. It serves as a source of protection and reassurance, allowing individuals to venture into the unknown while knowing that a secure attachment figure remains available for comfort and guidance during times of distress. In this way, the secure base acts as a buffer against anxiety and fear, fostering a sense of emotional resilience and self-assurance. Moreover, the secure base facilitates the development of trust and empathy, laying the groundwork for healthy relationship dynamics and social interactions.

The provision of a secure base nurtures the cultivation of autonomy and self-regulation. By having a secure foundation to return to as needed, individuals can gradually build their capacities to explore, learn, and grow independently, all while maintaining the fundamental security of a supportive attachment figure. This delicate balance between safety and autonomy is fundamental for the healthy progression of developmental milestones and the establishment of a robust sense of self.

The origins of the secure base phenomenon can be traced back to observations of infant-caregiver interactions, where the responsive and sensitive nature of the caregiver's support was found to significantly influence the child's ability to engage in exploration and learning. These early experiences form the basis for internal working models, shaping individuals' expectations of relationships and patterns of attachment throughout their lives.

2. Autonomy Development in the Context of Attachment:

Autonomy development encompasses the individual's ability to act independently and make decisions based on personal agency. In the context of attachment theory, autonomy development is i closely linked to the quality of early caregiving experiences and the establishment of secure attachment patterns. During infancy and early childhood, the gradual attainment of autonomy is closely intertwined with the child's exploration of the environment and the cultivation of a sense of mastery and competence. The interplay between the need for safety and the desire for independence shapes the trajectory of autonomy development within the framework of attachment. Secure attachments provide a foundation that fosters the child's confidence to undertake exploratory behaviors while knowing they have a safe haven to return to if needed. These early experiences form the basis for the development of a healthy balance between seeking support from caregivers and advancing towards autonomously-driven activities. Children with secure attachments tend to exhibit more resilience and self-assurance when approaching new experiences, as the secure base offered by their caregivers allows them to approach challenges with a greater sense of confidence. Conversely, insecure attachment patterns can impede autonomy development, leading to difficulties in managing separations, heightened anxiety during exploratory behavior, and limited initiative in independent decision-making. Understanding autonomy development within the context of attachment enables caregivers and professionals to appreciate the delicate balancing act required to support children in establishing a solid foundation of self-reliance while maintaining a secure base for reassurance and comfort. Recognizing the impact of early attachment experiences on autonomy development also underscores the significance of providing responsive and sensitive care, as these factors can significantly influence a child's developing sense of agency and autonomy.

3. The Conceprt of Balancing Safety with Exploration:

In the framework of attachment theory, the concept of balancing safety with exploration holds significant weight in understanding the dynamics of human development. Theoretical perspectives offer invaluable insights into the delicate equilibrium between seeking independence and the need for a secure base. One prominent theoretical framework is the evolutionary perspective, which posits that the inclination towards exploration is an adaptive trait honed through generations. This perspective emphasizes the role of the caregiver as a source of protection and support, allowing the individual to venture into unfamiliar territories with the confidence of a secure base to return to. Furthermore, it underscores the evolutionary advantage of balancing risk-taking behaviors with the comfort of a safe haven, fostering resilience and adaptability. Another influential perspective is the psychodynamic approach, delving into the interplay between internal drives and external influences. From this vantage point, the pursuit of exploration symbolizes the quest for autonomy and self-actualization, while the secure base represents the foundational support necessary for managing the complexities of the world. This perspective highlights the developmental significance of early attachments in shaping the individual's capacity for healthy exploration and independence. Additionally, the cognitive-behavioral perspective offers a lens through which the cognitive processes underlying the interplay of safety and exploration can be understood. It emphasizes how internal working models and cognitive schemas influence the individual's perception of safety and their propensity for exploring the environment. This perspective illuminates the critical role of early experiences in shaping the individual's beliefs about their abilities to seek new experiences while having a secure base to rely on.

4. The Interplay Between Dependency and Independence:

A fundamental aspect of attachment theory is understanding the delicate balance between dependency and independence within the context of human relationships. The interplay between these two constructs is crucial in shaping an individual's development and overall well-being. Dependency denotes the reliance on others for emotional support, validation, and security, while independence refers to the capacity to assert oneself, make autonomous decisions, and pursue personal goals. This dynamic interaction between dependency and independence is deeply rooted in the attachment system, as it reflects the dual nature of human needs for connection and autonomy.

Attachment theory posits that healthy psychological development involves the gradual transition from a state of complete dependency in infancy to achieving a sense of secure independence in adulthood. However, this transition is not linear or uniform across individuals, and the interplay between dependency and independence continues to evolve throughout the lifespan. Early experiences with caregivers significantly influence how individuals balance their dependence on others and their pursuit of autonomy. A secure attachment provides a safe foundation for individuals to explore and assert their independence, knowing that a supportive figure is available when needed. Conversely, insecure attachments may lead to either excessive dependency or avoidance of intimacy, hindering the development of healthy independence.

The interplay between dependency and independence is intimately linked to emotional regulation and self-esteem. Individuals with secure attachments tend to demonstrate better emotional regulation skills, allowing them to experience both dependency and independence without fear of abandonment or rejection. Conversely, those with insecure attachments may struggle to strike a balance, leading to periods of excessive dependency followed by attempts to overly assert independence as a defense mechanism.

Societal and cultural norms play a significant role in shaping the interplay between dependency and independence. Cultural expectations regarding interdependence within families or communities can influence individuals' attitudes toward seeking support versus pursuing autonomy. Moreover, gender norms and expectations can also impact how dependency and independence are perceived and expressed. Understanding these environmental influences is critical in comprehensively addressing the interplay between dependency and independence within attachment dynamics.

5. Environmental Influences on Exploration and Attachment:

The environment plays a crucial role in shaping the interplay between exploration and attachment in individuals. Environmental influences encompass a wide range of factors, including cultural norms, familial dynamics, socioeconomic status, and community structures. These influences can significantly impact an individual's capacity for autonomous exploration while maintaining secure attachment relationships. Cultural norms and practices shape the expectations and boundaries around exploration and attachment within a society. For example, cultures that prioritize independence may encourage early autonomy in children, while collectivist societies may emphasize interdependence and close familial ties. Such cultural differences can influence the development of attachment styles and the extent of exploratory behaviors permissible within these contexts.

Familial dynamics, particularly parent-child relationships, form the core foundation for attachment and exploration. Responsive and supportive caregiving fosters a sense of security that enables children to venture into their surroundings with confidence, knowing they have a safe haven to return to if needed.

Conversely, inconsistent or neglectful caregiving can hinder a child's exploration and impede the formation of secure attachments. Furthermore, socioeconomic status can impact access to resources, opportunities for exploration, and the quality of attachment experiences. Children from higher socioeconomic backgrounds may benefit from enriched environments that facilitate exploration, whereas those facing economic adversity might encounter barriers to autonomous discovery.

Community structures also exert influence, as the availability of safe and stimulating environments can either promote or hinder exploration. Access to safe outdoor spaces, recreational facilities, and educational resources can either fuel or restrict exploration opportunities for individuals. Additionally, social support networks within communities contribute to the formation of secure attachments by providing emotional validation, guidance, and a sense of belonging for individuals undertaking their exploratory journeys.

6. Challenges in Achieving Autonomy Within Secure Attachments:

Achieving autonomy within secure attachments presents a multifaceted challenge for both children and caregivers. While secure attachments provide a foundation of safety and support, the process of fostering autonomy can encounter various hurdles. One significant challenge lies in finding the delicate balance between encouraging independence and maintaining a secure base. Caregivers may struggle with allowing children to explore and take risks while ensuring their safety and well-being. Furthermore, children may experience conflicts between their desire for autonomy and the comfort of the familiar attachment figure, leading to inner turmoil and ambivalence. Additionally, societal expectations and cultural norms can impose constraints on the expression of autonomy within the context of secure attachments. These external pressures can complicate the pursuit of autonomy development within the attachment framework. Moreover, as children strive for independence, they may encounter internal resistance stemming from their attachment dynamics, such as guilt or fear of jeopardizing the secure relationship. This internal conflict can impede the natural progression toward autonomy and may require intentional guidance and support from caregivers. Another crucial challenge in achieving autonomy within secure attachments is recognizing that autonomy does not equate to emotional detachment. It is essential to emphasize that autonomy development occurs within the context of emotional connectedness and relational security. Nurturing this understanding can prevent misunderstandings and misconceptions surrounding the pursuit of independence within the attachment system. Moreover, maintaining open communication and trust within the caregiver-child relationship is essential for managing the challenges of autonomy development. Striking a balance between providing support and allowing freedom of exploration demands consistent effort and flexibility. Despite these challenges, fostering autonomy within secure attachments is vital for promoting healthy development and resilience.

7. Implications for Caregivers - Strategies Promoting Balanced Growth:

Caregivers play a pivotal role in shaping the development of children, particularly in fostering secure attachments and promoting balanced growth. Understanding the implications of attachment theory on caregiving practices is crucial for creating an environment that nurtures exploration, security, and independence in children.

First and foremost, it is essential for caregivers to provide a secure base from which children can venture out to explore the world. By offering a safe and supportive environment, caregivers lay the foundation for children to develop a sense of competence and autonomy. Encouraging exploration while being available as a source of comfort and safety creates a secure attachment, instilling confidence in children to gradually expand their boundaries.

Fostering autonomy in children involves respecting their choices and providing opportunities for decision-making within appropriate limits. Caregivers can empower children by allowing them to make age-appropriate choices and take ownership of their actions, thereby reinforcing a sense of independence. This approach not only encourages self-reliance but also strengthens the bond between caregivers and children, as it acknowledges the child's individuality and agency.

In line with attachment theory, responsive caregiving is paramount in promoting balanced growth. Caregivers need to be attuned to the emotional needs of children, offering support and reassurance when they encounter challenges during their exploratory pursuits. Demonstrating sensitivity to children's cues and emotions fosters a secure attachment, nurturing resilience and emotional regulation. By providing a dependable presence, caregivers facilitate the development of a strong internal working model, enhancing children's capacity to form healthy relationships and cope with stress throughout their lives.

Creating a nurturing environment that emphasizes open communication and validation of children's experiences is instrumental in promoting balanced growth. Caregivers should strive to establish a culture of trust and understanding, where children feel comfortable expressing their thoughts and feelings. By acknowledging and validating their experiences, caregivers affirm children's emotions and perspectives, fostering a secure attachment that cultivates a healthy sense of self-worth and emotional well-being.

Lastly, caregivers should recognize the significance of their own well-being in promoting balanced growth in children. Self-care is integral in maintaining the emotional availability and responsiveness necessary for fostering secure attachments. Building a support network, seeking guidance when needed, and prioritizing their own mental and emotional health equips caregivers with the capacity to provide the nurturing environment essential for supporting children's exploration, security, and independence.

Proximity Maintenance and Safe Haven

1. Historical Perspectives on Proximity Seeking Behaviors:

Throughout history, the study of proximity seeking behaviors has been influenced by a variety of disciplines, including psychology, ethology, and evolutionary biology. The origins of these behaviors can be traced back to the early work of renowned ethologists such as Konrad Lorenz and Nikolaas Tinbergen, who observed and documented the instinctual tendencies of young animals to seek proximity to their caregivers for safety and security. These pioneering observations laid the foundation for understanding the innate nature of proximity seeking behaviors in both human and non-human species.

In the field of psychology, the concept of attachment theory, developed by John Bowlby in the mid-20th century, provided a groundbreaking framework for comprehending the historical roots of proximity seeking behaviors. Bowlby's theory emphasized the adaptive significance of proximity maintenance and safe haven provision as fundamental components of the attachment system. Moreover, Bowlby drew upon insights from psychoanalysis, cognitive psychology, and developmental psychology to construct a comprehensive model of attachment that integrated historical perspectives on proximity seeking behaviors.

The historical evolution of research on proximity seeking behaviors also extends to cross-cultural studies, where anthropologists and sociologists have investigated how different societal norms and caregiving practices shape the manifestation of attachment-related behaviors. Cross-cultural research has revealed that while the fundamental motives of proximity maintenance are universal, the specific forms and expressions of these behaviors vary across diverse cultural contexts. By exploring historical and cultural factors, scholars have gained valuable insights into the adaptive and contextual nature of proximity seeking behaviors.

Historical perspectives on proximity seeking behaviors have expanded through the emergence of neuroscience and neurobiology, which have delved into the underlying neural mechanisms and brain circuits associated with attachment-related processes. The integration of neuroscientific findings with historical understandings provides a multidimensional view of proximity seeking behaviors, elucidating the interplay between biological predispositions and environmental influences in shaping attachment dynamics.

2. Mechanisms of Proximity Maintenance in Early Childhood:

In early childhood, the mechanisms of proximity maintenance play a crucial role in the development of attachment bonds. Children rely on these mechanisms to ensure closeness and connection with their primary caregivers, who serve as the source of security and comfort. One fundamental mechanism is the use of proximity-seeking behaviors, where children actively seek physical closeness to their attachment figures. This may involve reaching out for contact, clinging, or following the caregiver from room to room. Additionally, nonverbal cues such as eye contact, facial expressions, and gestures are employed to maintain proximity. Through these behaviors, children establish a sense of safety and predictability in their environment.

Young children often exhibit separation protest as a means of maintaining proximity. When separated from their attachment figures, they may display distress and cry out in an attempt to regain the closeness they desire. This innate response reflects the importance of proximity maintenance in early childhood and highlights the emotional significance of attachment relationships.

Another key aspect of proximity maintenance in early childhood is the concept of symbolic security objects, such as a favorite blanket or stuffed animal. These items serve as transitional objects that provide children with a sense of continuity and security, allowing them to maintain proximity even in the absence of their primary caregivers. The presence of these objects can mitigate feelings of distress and anxiety, offering children a tangible representation of the secure base provided by their caregivers.

The establishment of routines and rituals contributes to the maintenance of proximity in early childhood. Familiar daily activities, such as bedtime routines, meal times, and playtime, create a sense of predictability and security for children. These routines not only facilitate proximity maintenance but also promote a supportive and nurturing environment, reinforcing the attachment bond between child and caregiver.

Understanding the mechanisms of proximity maintenance in early childhood is essential for comprehending the foundation of attachment relationships. It underscores the significance of these early experiences in shaping the emotional landscape of individuals, laying the groundwork for future social and emotional development. Recognizing the varied ways in which children maintain proximity provides valuable insights into the dynamics of attachment and informs strategies for promoting secure attachment relationships in early childhood settings.

3. The Role of Attachment Figures in Providing a Safe Haven:

Within the framework of attachment behaviors, the concept of a 'safe haven' refers to the function of the attachment figure in providing a source of comfort, protection, and soothing when the individual experiences negative emotions or encounters stressful situations. The presence of the attachment figure serves as a secure base from which the individual can explore the world, knowing that there is a reliable source of support to return to in times of need.

Central to the provision of a safe haven is the quality of the attachment relationship. Secure attachment figures are responsive, emotionally available, and attuned to the needs of the individual. When a person feels distressed, they seek proximity to the attachment figure with the expectation of finding solace and reassurance. This process fosters a sense of security and emotional regulation, laying the foundation for healthy coping mechanisms and resilience in the face of adversity.

The role of the attachment figure in providing a safe haven evolves over the course of development. In early childhood, this role is typically fulfilled by primary caregivers such as parents or guardians. As individuals grow, the scope of attachment figures may expand to include other significant figures such as siblings, friends, or romantic partners. Additionally, the ability to provide a safe haven extends beyond mere physical presence; it encompasses the emotional availability and responsiveness of the attachment figure, which significantly influences the individual's sense of safety and well-being.

Notably, the quality of the safe haven provided by attachment figures has far-reaching implications for psychological and emotional development. Research indicates that individuals who have experienced consistent and supportive safe haven experiences tend to exhibit greater resilience, adaptability, and emotional regulation skills. Conversely, inadequate or unreliable safe haven provision can contribute to increased vulnerability to stress, anxiety, and maladaptive coping strategies.

4. Contextual Influences on Proximity Maintenance:

Proximity maintenance, as a fundamental aspect of attachment behavior, is influenced by various contextual factors that shape the dynamics of human relationships. Understanding these influences is crucial in comprehending the complexities and nuances of attachment processes. Contextual factors encompass a wide range of elements, including cultural, environmental, and relational aspects that play pivotal roles in shaping behaviors related to proximity seeking and safe haven provision.

Cultural influences significantly impact how individuals perceive and express their attachment needs. Cultural norms, beliefs, and practices guide the manifestation of proximity maintenance behaviors within a specific society. For instance, cultures that prioritize interdependence and collective harmony may emphasize closeness and availability of attachment figures, fostering robust proximity maintenance behaviors. In contrast, cultures valuing independence and autonomy may shape attachment dynamics towards greater self-reliance, impacting the utilization of safe havens and proximity seeking.

The environmental context also holds considerable sway over proximity maintenance. Socioeconomic conditions, neighborhood safety, and access to resources can influence the availability and effectiveness of safe havens. In environments marked by instability or insecurity, individuals may demonstrate heightened proximity maintenance behaviors as a means of seeking security and reassurance. Moreover, the physical layout of living spaces and the presence of supportive social networks can either facilitate or impede proximity seeking behaviors, underscoring the environmental impact on attachment dynamics.

Relational influences, particularly within familial and caregiving contexts, significantly shape proximity maintenance patterns. The quality of interactions with attachment figures, such as caregivers and close family members, profoundly impacts an individual's inclination to seek proximity and utilize safe havens. Secure and responsive caregiving fosters a sense of trust and comfort, promoting adaptive proximity maintenance behaviors, whereas insecure or inconsistent caregiving may lead to disruptions in proximity seeking and reliance on safe havens.

Additionally, psychosocial factors, including individual differences and personal experiences, contribute to the contextual landscape of proximity maintenance. Attachment histories, past relational traumas, and coping strategies all intersect with contextual influences, shaping the ways in which individuals engage in proximity seeking and safe haven utilization.

5. Implications for Clinical Practice:

Understanding the dynamics of attachment can significantly inform therapeutic interventions, particularly in the domain of mental health and relational issues. By integrating the tenets of attachment theory into clinical practice, professionals can gain valuable insights into the developmental roots of emotional and interpersonal difficulties in their clients.

One of the key implications for clinical practice is the recognition of the significance of early attachment relationships in shaping individuals' emotional regulation capacities and responses to stress. Therapists can utilize this understanding to help clients explore and make sense of their attachment history, which may underpin their present-day struggles with intimacy, trust, and vulnerability. In doing so, therapists can foster a safe therapeutic environment that mirrors the secure base and safe haven provided by caregivers in attachment theory.

Additionally, attachment theory underscores the importance of the therapeutic relationship as a vehicle for healing and change. By embodying secure attachment principles such as attunement, empathy, and nonjudgmental acceptance, clinicians can model healthy relational dynamics and facilitate corrective emotional experiences for their clients. This can be particularly impactful for individuals who have experienced early attachment disruptions or trauma, offering them the opportunity to develop secure attachments within the therapeutic dyad.

The application of attachment theory in clinical practice extends to interventions aimed at addressing relational difficulties within couples and families. By unpacking the attachment dynamics at play within these systems, therapists can guide clients in recognizing and modifying maladaptive patterns of interaction. Through promoting communication strategies that foster proximity-seeking and safe haven behaviors, therapists can assist individuals and families in cultivating more secure and fulfilling relational bonds.

Importantly, the implications of attachment theory for clinical practice also highlight the need for a nuanced understanding of attachment patterns across the lifespan. Recognizing that attachment dynamics evolve and manifest differently in various developmental stages, clinicians can tailor their interventions to meet the unique attachment-related needs of children, adolescents, adults, and older adults.

Emotional Regulation

1. Biological Underpinnings:

Emotional regulation, a complex and dynamic process, is rooted in the interplay of biological systems within the human body. At the core of emotional regulation are the workings of the nervous system, particularly the autonomic nervous system (ANS) and the central nervous system (CNS). The ANS, comprising the sympathetic and parasympathetic branches, plays a pivotal role in orchestrating the physiological responses to emotional stimuli. The sympathetic branch, often associated with the 'fight or flight' response, primes the body for action during times of perceived threat or stress, while the parasympathetic branch helps restore the body to a state of calm after the threat has passed. Within the CNS, the limbic system, notably the amygdala and hippocampus, serves as the epicenter for emotion processing and regulation. The amygdala, in particular, is instrumental in evaluating the emotional salience of stimuli and initiating appropriate physiological and behavioral responses.

The interplay between neurotransmitters and hormones complexly modulate emotional reactivity and regulation. Neurotransmitters like serotonin, dopamine, and norepinephrine are implicated in regulating mood, arousal, and reward processing, thus influencing emotional states and regulatory processes. Additionally, the endocrine system, particularly the release of cortisol by the adrenal glands in response to stress, contributes to the modulation of emotional responses. Notably, the hypothalamic-pituitary-adrenal (HPA) axis, a key component of the stress response, interacts closely with the ANS to regulate emotional reactivity and coping strategies.

The burgeoning field of epigenetics has also uncovered the influence of genetic and environmental factors on emotional regulation. Research suggests that early life experiences, such as caregiving quality and attachment relationships, can shape the expression of genes related to stress reactivity and emotional regulation, thereby sculpting individuals' emotional responsiveness throughout their lifespan. Moreover, the ongoing interplay between genetic predispositions and environmental influences underscores the plasticity of emotional regulation and the potential for targeted interventions to enhance individuals' regulatory capacities.

2. The Role of Attachment in Developing Emotional Self-Regulation:

Attachment theory emphasizes the significant influence of early relationships, particularly those with primary caregivers, on the development of emotional self-regulation. Through the lens of attachment theory, emotional self-regulation is viewed as a critical adaptive skill that enables individuals to modulate their emotional experiences and expressions in response to internal and external stimuli.

Central to the role of attachment in developing emotional self-regulation is the concept of secure attachment. Securely attached children tend to have caregivers who are consistently responsive, empathetic, and attuned to their emotional needs. As a result, these children learn to trust the availability and responsiveness of their caregivers in times of distress, facilitating the development of effective emotion regulation strategies. Such children are more likely to explore their surroundings confidently, knowing they have a secure base to return to when needed, fostering emotional resilience and adaptive coping mechanisms.

Conversely, insecure attachment patterns, such as ambivalent, avoidant, or disorganized attachments, can impede the development of optimal emotional self-regulation. Children with insecure attachments may struggle to regulate their emotions effectively, often exhibiting difficulties in managing stress, expressing their needs, or seeking comfort from others. These challenges stem from inconsistent or inadequate caregiving experiences, which may lead to the internalization of maladaptive regulatory patterns.

Attachment styles significantly impact the way individuals perceive and respond to emotional cues in their interactions with others. For instance, individuals with anxious-preoccupied attachment tendencies may exhibit heightened reactivity to emotional triggers, experiencing difficulties in downregulating intense emotions. In contrast, those with dismissive-avoidant attachment patterns may habitually suppress or minimize emotional expressions, leading to emotional detachment and discomfort with intimacy.

The multifaceted interplay between attachment and emotional self-regulation extends beyond childhood, shaping individuals' relational dynamics, interpersonal conflict resolution, and overall well-being in adulthood. Recognizing the influence of early attachment experiences is pivotal in understanding the complexities of emotional regulation across the lifespan and underscores the significance of secure attachment as a foundational pillar for adaptive self-regulatory capacities.

3. Attachment Styles and Their Impact on Emotional Responses:

Attachment theory proposes that early experiences with caregivers shape an individual's attachment style, which in turn influences emotional responses throughout life. There are four primary attachment styles identified: secure, anxious-preoccupied, dismissive-avoidant, and fearful-avoidant. These styles develop based on the consistency and sensitivity of caregiving received during infancy and childhood. A secure attachment style is associated with a positive view of oneself and others, leading to balanced emotional regulation and healthy interpersonal relationships. In contrast, the anxious-preoccupied attachment style often results from inconsistent caregiving, leading to heightened emotional reactivity, anxiety, and a constant need for validation and reassurance. Conversely, individuals with a dismissive-avoidant attachment style tend to downplay their emotions and exhibit self-reliance, often due to caregiver unresponsiveness or rejection. Lastly, the fearful-avoidant attachment style stems from experiences of inconsistent or abusive caregiving, resulting in a mix of both anxious and avoidant behaviors in relationships. Understanding these attachment styles provides insight into how individuals approach and respond to emotional stimuli in various contexts. Research has demonstrated that individuals with secure attachment styles are generally more resilient in managing stress and regulating emotions, while those with insecure attachment styles may struggle with emotional dysregulation and have difficulty forming and maintaining stable relationships. Furthermore, attachment styles can impact how individuals interpret and respond to social cues, manage conflict, and seek emotional support.

4. Caregiver Influences - Dynamics of Co-regulation and Autonomy:

Caregivers play a pivotal role in shaping a child's emotional regulation skills within the framework of attachment theory. The dynamics of co-regulation and autonomy are essential components of this process. Co-regulation refers to the interactive process through which caregivers and children manage emotions together, providing crucial scaffolding for the child's developing self-regulatory abilities. Caregivers serve as external regulators, offering support and guidance to help children manage their emotional experiences. This co-regulatory process involves sensitive responsiveness to the child's emotional cues, validation of their feelings, and providing a safe space for expression. Through consistent co-regulation, children gradually internalize these regulatory processes, leading to the development of autonomous emotional regulation skills. This gradual shift from external to internal regulation is critical for fostering independence and resilience in children. Autonomy in emotional regulation allows children to regulate their emotions independently while drawing upon the secure base provided by their caregivers. Caregivers support the development of autonomy by gradually encouraging children to take increasing responsibility for their emotional regulation, while still being available as a source of comfort and support when needed. This delicate balance between providing autonomy and remaining accessible as a secure base is crucial for promoting healthy emotional regulation. Furthermore, caregivers' own emotional regulation capabilities significantly influence the co-regulation process. Caregivers who model effective emotion regulation strategies provide a valuable template for children to learn from and emulate. Conversely, caregivers who struggle with regulating their own emotions may inadvertently impart maladaptive regulation strategies to their children. Understanding the interconnected dynamics of co-regulation and autonomy sheds light on the profound impact caregivers have on their children's emotional development within the attachment framework.

5. Maladaptive Regulation Strategies and Attachment Insecurities:

Maladaptive regulation strategies refer to the ineffective or damaging ways in which individuals attempt to manage their emotions within the framework of attachment. These strategies often stem from attachment insecurities that have developed from early interactions with caregivers. Such insecurities can manifest in various forms, including anxious preoccupation, avoidance of emotional intimacy, or disorganized patterns of attachment. Individuals with these insecurities may resort to maladaptive regulation strategies as an attempt to cope with their underlying fears of rejection, abandonment, or engulfment.

One common maladaptive regulation strategy is emotional suppression, where individuals attempt to bury or ignore their emotions in an effort to maintain a sense of control or avoid perceived vulnerability. While this may provide temporary relief, long-term suppression can lead to heightened stress, exacerbated emotional distress, and strained interpersonal relationships. Another maladaptive strategy is emotional numbing, wherein individuals detach themselves from their feelings as a defense mechanism against potential hurt or disappointment. This can hinder the development of close, meaningful connections and impede the ability to engage in mutually fulfilling relationships.

Maladaptive regulation strategies can take the form of externalizing behaviors such as aggression, substance abuse, or risk-taking activities, all of which serve as methods to distract from or alleviate emotional pain. These behaviors can offer fleeting relief but often contribute to a cycle of emotional dysregulation and negative outcomes. Additionally, individuals may engage in self-sabotaging behaviors, seeking validation and reassurance in destructive ways that further perpetuate their attachment insecurities.

Attachment insecurities also play a significant role in the formation of maladaptive coping mechanisms, including catastrophizing, rumination, and cognitive distortions that amplify negative emotions and undermine resilience. These patterns of thinking can exacerbate emotional distress and lead to a self-perpetuating cycle of maladaptive regulation. Furthermore, individuals with attachment insecurities may struggle with boundary setting and experience challenges in effectively communicating their emotional needs, leading to difficulties in establishing and maintaining healthy relationships.

6. Interpersonal Relationships - Safe Havens for Emotional Expression:

Interpersonal relationships serve as a primary source of support and validation, offering individuals a secure base from which to explore and regulate their emotional experiences. The presence of a trusted caregiver or close relationship figure can significantly impact an individual's ability to effectively manage and express emotions, thus influencing overall well-being and psychological adjustment.

First and foremost, secure attachments foster a sense of safety and security, providing individuals with the confidence to openly express their emotions without fear of rejection or invalidation. By establishing an environment of trust and acceptance, caregivers and significant others create a space where individuals feel comfortable sharing their innermost feelings, thoughts, and vulnerabilities. This open emotional dialogue forms the cornerstone of healthy emotional regulation, as it allows individuals to process and make sense of their experiences within a supportive relationship framework.

Interpersonal relationships offer a platform for co-regulation, wherein individuals draw upon the emotional support and guidance of their attachment figures to manage intense or distressing emotions. Through empathic responses, active listening, and mutual understanding, caregivers and close relationships help individuals regulate their emotional states, fostering a sense of balance and stability. In doing so, these interactions lay the groundwork for the development of adaptive emotion regulation strategies, enabling individuals to cope effectively with life's challenges and stressors.

Additionally, the safe haven provided by interpersonal relationships serves as a buffer against the adverse effects of emotional dysregulation and distress. By having access to a supportive network, individuals can seek comfort, reassurance, and perspective during times of heightened emotional arousal or adversity. This fosters resilience and emotional strength, as individuals are better equipped to weather difficult circumstances when they feel unconditionally supported and understood by their attachment figures.

The reciprocal nature of emotional expression within interpersonal relationships cultivates a deeper sense of intimacy and connection. When individuals are able to authentically express their emotions and have them validated by their attachment figures, it facilitates a profound bond of understanding and empathy. This shared emotional experience contributes to the relational depth and closeness, reinforcing the role of safe havens as nurturing environments for emotional expression and regulation.

7. Cognitive Processes in Emotion Regulation:

When individuals encounter emotionally challenging situations, their cognitive appraisal and interpretation of those experiences significantly influence their emotional responses and subsequent regulatory efforts. At the core of cognitive processes in emotion regulation lies the concept of reappraisal, wherein individuals reinterpret the meaning of distressing events or stimuli to modulate their emotional reactions. By engaging in cognitive reappraisal, individuals can effectively down-regulate negative emotions and promote adaptive coping strategies. Furthermore, cognitive flexibility, the ability to shift perspectives and consider alternative explanations, contributes to enhanced emotion regulation capacities.

The development of metacognitive skills, such as self-awareness and attentional control, significantly influences individuals' capacity to regulate their emotions. Metacognition enables individuals to monitor their internal states, recognize emotional triggers, and employ cognitive strategies to modulate affective experiences. Additionally, executive functions encompassing working memory, inhibitory control, and cognitive flexibility play a crucial role in regulating emotional impulses and orchestrating adaptive responses in emotionally charged scenarios.

The role of cognitive biases in emotion regulation cannot be understated. Individuals' cognitive schemas and information processing tendencies shape their interpretations of social cues, interpersonal interactions, and attachment-related experiences. These cognitive biases may predispose individuals to adopt maladaptive regulatory strategies, fostering disruptions in emotional regulation processes.

Examining the developmental trajectories of cognitive processes in emotion regulation unveils the progressive refinement of these abilities across the lifespan. Children initially rely on external scaffolding from caregivers to support their developing cognitive regulation capacities. As they mature, the integration of complex cognitive processes enhances their autonomy in managing emotional experiences and managing interpersonal dynamics.

As our understanding of the interconnections between cognitive processes and emotion regulation continues to evolve, interventions aimed at bolstering cognitive reappraisal skills, metacognitive awareness, and executive functions hold promise in cultivating resilient emotion regulation capabilities.

8. Developmental Trajectories of Emotion Regulation:

Infants rely heavily on external regulation by their primary caregivers, gradually transitioning to more internalized forms of regulation as they grow and develop. The early interactions with caregivers serve as the foundation for the development of emotion regulation abilities. As children move into the preschool years, they begin to display increasing autonomy in their emotions and behavior, although they still require guidance and support from significant others. The school-age years mark a period of continued refinement in emotion regulation skills, as children learn to recognize and label their emotions while also acquiring strategies for managing them effectively. Adolescence brings about unique challenges, as individuals manage the complexities of identity formation, peer relationships, and emotional self-regulation amidst biological and social changes. Emotion dysregulation during this stage can have significant implications for mental health and well-being. Furthermore, the transition into adulthood involves further consolidation of emotion regulation abilities, influenced by factors such as life experiences, relationships, and coping strategies. The developmental trajectories of emotion regulation are also shaped by individual differences in temperament, attachment styles, and environmental influences. Understanding these trajectories is essential for promoting healthy emotion regulation across the lifespan.

Characteristics of Secure Attachment - Stability and Resilience

1. Introduction to Secure Attachment:

Secure attachment, a fundamental concept in attachment theory, represents an individual's ability to form healthy and enduring emotional bonds with caregivers or significant others. It serves as a cornerstone in understanding the dynamics of human relationships and psychological well-being. At its core, secure attachment reflects a consistent sense of trust, safety, and comfort that an individual experiences in their interactions with attachment figures. The establishment of secure attachment is rooted in the responsiveness and sensitivity of caregivers, as it lays the groundwork for emotional security and resilience. This form of attachment provides a solid base from which individuals can explore the world, seek social support, and regulate their emotions effectively. Recognized as a key determinant of socioemotional development, secure attachment contributes to positive self-esteem, adaptive coping strategies, and the capacity to form healthy relationships. Moreover, secure attachment acts as a protective factor against stress and adversity, fostering resilience and psychological well-being.

2. The Pillars of Stability in Secure Attachment:

Stability in secure attachment is underpinned by several defining pillars that form the bedrock of emotional security and resilience. These pillars serve as the foundational elements that contribute to the durability and steadfastness of secure attachments across diverse contexts and relationships. One pivotal pillar is the establishment of a consistent and attuned caregiver-infant relationship during early development. This entails the caregiver's ability to sensitively respond to the infant's cues, thereby fostering a sense of predictability and reliability in the child's environment.

Additionally, the cultivation of a secure base, as proposed by attachment theory, plays a crucial role in maintaining stability. Through the provision of a secure base, individuals feel empowered to explore their surroundings while having the reassurance of a safe haven to return to in times of distress. Furthermore, clear and effective communication within attachment relationships serves as another essential pillar of stability. Open and transparent dialogue fosters understanding, empathy, and mutual support, thereby solidifying the foundation of secure attachments. Another significant pillar is the promotion of positive internal working models, which influence individuals' perceptions of themselves, others, and relationships. Healthy internal working models contribute to emotional stability and adaptive coping strategies in the face of challenges or adversities. Moreover, the mutual cultivation of trust and dependability between attachment figures and individuals significantly contributes to the stability of secure attachments. This trust forms the cornerstone of resilient and enduring relationships, providing a sense of safety and security. Finally, the integration of mindfulness and emotional regulation practices within the framework of secure attachments reinforces stability by promoting self-awareness, stress management, and overall well-being. These interconnected pillars collectively uphold the stability of secure attachment, forming a sturdy and reliable foundation for individuals to manage the complexities of human relationships and emotional experiences.

3. Resilience Development Through Secure Bonds:

Secure attachment plays a pivotal role in fostering resilience and psychological well-being across the lifespan. Research indicates that individuals with secure attachment styles are more likely to develop effective coping mechanisms, emotional regulation skills, and a positive outlook on life, which contribute to their ability to overcome challenges and adversities. The foundation of resilience development through secure bonds lies in the consistent and nurturing care provided by primary caregivers during early childhood. Children who experience responsive and emotionally attuned interactions with their caregivers are better equipped to develop a sense of security, self-esteem, and confidence in their abilities to manage stress and regulate complex emotions. Additionally, the presence of a secure base enables individuals to seek support and effectively utilize resources during times of distress, further enhancing their capacity for resilience. Furthermore, secure attachments promote the formation of internal working models that influence how individuals perceive and respond to stressful situations. These internalized representations guide their problem-solving strategies, decision-making processes, and the interpretation of social cues, contributing to adaptive and resilient behavior. In adult relationships, individuals with secure attachment styles demonstrate greater interpersonal competence, empathy, and cooperation, which further bolster their capacity to endure and rebound from life's challenges. Moreover, the stability and predictability offered by secure attachments provide a strong buffer against the detrimental effects of traumatic experiences, contributing to improved mental health outcomes and overall well-being. Understanding the link between secure attachment and resilience has significant implications for therapeutic interventions and support systems aimed at promoting psychological strength and recovery.

4. Emotional Regulation and Secure Attachment:

Emotional regulation involves the ability to understand, manage, and express one's emotions in a constructive manner. Individuals with secure attachments often demonstrate a higher degree of emotional regulation, which contributes to their overall well-being and positive interpersonal relationships.

Securely attached individuals are more adept at recognizing and labeling their emotions, allowing them to effectively communicate their feelings to others. This self-awareness enables them to seek appropriate support when needed and manage social interactions with greater ease. Moreover, secure attachment provides a sense of emotional security, fostering an environment where individuals feel comfortable exploring and expressing their emotions.

Emotional regulation within secure attachments is closely linked to stress management. Research suggests that individuals with secure attachments exhibit a more adaptive stress response, enabling them to cope with challenging situations more effectively. This resilience in the face of adversity stems from the consistent emotional support and validation experienced within secure attachment relationships.

In addition, secure attachment fosters the development of healthy coping strategies, allowing individuals to regulate their emotions in a manner that promotes psychological well-being. By internalizing supportive experiences within secure relationships, individuals can draw upon these positive interactions to manage stressful circumstances and regulate their emotional responses.

Emotional regulation within secure attachments has far-reaching implications for mental health. Studies have indicated that individuals with secure attachments are less susceptible to anxiety and depression, highlighting the protective role of secure attachment in promoting emotional well-being.

5. Trust Formation and Its Role in Security:

Within the context of attachment theory, trust is established through consistent and responsive caregiving, enabling the child to develop a sense of predictability and safety in their relationships. This sense of trust becomes internalized as a working model that shapes future interactions and expectations.

Securely attached individuals tend to have experienced caregivers who consistently met their needs, demonstrating reliability and attunement to their emotions. As a result, these individuals develop a core belief that others are generally trustworthy and dependable, fostering a positive outlook on relationships and the world around them.

The establishment of trust in early childhood serves as a fundamental precursor to the sense of security found in secure attachments. Trust enables individuals to feel confident in seeking support and comfort from others, knowing that their emotional expressions will be acknowledged and validated. This emotional validation further solidifies the bond between the attachment figure and the individual, reinforcing the belief that their needs will be met in times of distress.

Trust formation within secure attachments contributes to the development of effective emotion regulation strategies. When individuals feel secure in their relationships, they are better equipped to express and manage their emotions in a healthy manner. The presence of a reliable attachment figure allows for the processing of challenging experiences, promoting adaptive coping mechanisms and reducing the likelihood of maladaptive responses to stressors.

In addition to its immediate impact, trust formation within secure attachments has long-lasting implications for interpersonal relationships and overall well-being. Individuals with a strong foundation of trust are more likely to form secure and supportive connections throughout their lives, as they approach interactions with an inherent belief in others' goodwill and reliability. This positive outlook fosters healthier relationships and contributes to a greater sense of fulfillment and connectedness.

6. Impact of Secure Attachment on Personality Development:

Personality development is closely linked with early attachment experiences, especially those characterized by security and stability. Children who experience secure attachment with their primary caregivers tend to develop a more resilient and adaptive personality over time. Securely attached individuals exhibit characteristics such as high self-esteem, emotional regulation, and the ability to form trusting relationships, all of which play a critical role in shaping their personality. The consistent and responsive care provided by primary caregivers fosters a sense of security and confidence in children, laying the foundation for healthy personality development. Securely attached individuals are more likely to possess a positive self-image and a strong sense of self-worth, attributes that contribute to their overall psychological well-being. Furthermore, they are often better equipped to manage stress and handle challenging situations, reflecting an enhanced capacity for robust personality development. Research indicates that individuals with a secure attachment history are more likely to display empathy, compassion, and prosocial behavior, reflecting the socio-emotional competence cultivated through their early attachment experiences. These individuals tend to exhibit greater resilience in the face of adversity, demonstrating an ability to bounce back from setbacks and maintain a balanced emotional state. Additionally, secure attachment contributes to the development of effective coping strategies and problem-solving skills, enabling individuals to confront life's challenges with optimism and confidence. As they mature, securely attached individuals often exhibit secure and trusting patterns of relating to others, fostering harmonious interpersonal interactions and forming meaningful connections. Their ability to establish and maintain supportive relationships underscores the profound impact of secure attachment on their personality development. By nurturing a sense of security, warmth, and responsiveness, secure attachments pave the way for the cultivation of a well-rounded and adaptive personality that serves as a cornerstone for future success and fulfillment.

7. The Influence of Secure Attachments on Social Competencies:

The foundations laid by secure attachments during early developmental stages have far-reaching implications for an individual's ability to form and maintain healthy relationships, communicate effectively, empathize with others, and manage social interactions. Research indicates that individuals with a history of secure attachments are more likely to exhibit higher levels of social competence, characterized by their ability to establish and sustain meaningful connections, resolve conflicts constructively, and adapt to diverse social environments.

One key aspect of the influence of secure attachments on social competencies is the development of emotional regulation skills. Children who experience secure attachments with caregivers learn to manage their emotions effectively, which forms the basis for their ability to regulate emotional responses in social settings. This foundational skill contributes to their capacity to approach social interactions with a sense of emotional security, enabling them to express themselves authentically and engage with others in a positive manner.

The influence of secure attachments extends to the development of empathy and perspective-taking abilities. Individuals who have experienced consistent and nurturing relationships in their early years are more likely to demonstrate empathy towards others and comprehend different perspectives. This enhanced empathic capacity fosters deeper and more meaningful connections, as it enables individuals to relate to others' experiences, understand their emotions, and offer support in times of need. Furthermore, the presence of secure attachments is associated with heightened social awareness, allowing individuals to manage complex social situations with sensitivity and insight.

In addition to emotional regulation and empathy, secure attachments contribute to the formation of trust and intimacy in relationships. Individuals who have internalized secure attachment models tend to approach social interactions with a sense of trust and openness. This inclination towards trusting others and forming secure bonds cultivates healthier, more fulfilling relationships, as individuals feel secure in expressing vulnerabilities and sharing experiences without fear of judgment or abandonment. Such interpersonal dynamics built on trust and intimacy facilitate deeper connections and foster a supportive social network, which further enhances an individual's overall social competencies.

8. Secure Attachment and Adaptive Coping Mechanisms:

Individuals with secure attachment styles are more likely to develop adaptive coping mechanisms that enable them to effectively manage life's challenges. Securely attached individuals tend to exhibit a greater sense of self-efficacy and resilience when encountering stressors, allowing them to approach difficulties with a proactive mindset.

One of the key adaptive coping mechanisms observed in those with secure attachment is problem-focused coping. This approach involves actively addressing the underlying issues and devising constructive solutions. Research has shown that individuals with secure attachments demonstrate a propensity for problem-solving and seeking social support when faced with adversity. By engaging in collaborative problem-solving and drawing on their secure base, these individuals are better equipped to manage stressful situations.

Individuals with secure attachment styles often exhibit effective emotion-focused coping strategies. They display emotional regulation and expression, enabling them to process and adapt to challenging circumstances without being overwhelmed by negative emotions. This emotional resilience reflects the secure foundation established during early attachment relationships, contributing to their ability to maintain psychological well-being in the face of adversity.

Additionally, secure attachment fosters a positive internal working model that shapes individuals' perceptions of themselves and others. This cognitive framework influences their interpretations of experiences, allowing them to maintain a balanced perspective even in difficult times. As a result, securely attached individuals are inclined to interpret setbacks as temporary and manageable, cultivating an optimistic outlook that facilitates adaptive coping.

The presence of secure attachment is linked to the development of effective stress management skills. Individuals with secure attachments tend to exhibit lower reactivity to stress and faster physiological recovery following stressful events. This enhanced ability to regulate stress responses contributes to their overall capacity to cope with challenging situations in a healthy and adaptive manner.

Behavioral Manifestations in Secure Attachments Across the Lifespan

1. Early Childhood - Foundation of Secure Interactions:

During early childhood, the foundation of secure interactions is established through a multitude of significant experiences and influences. Infants and young children rely heavily on their caregivers to meet their physical and emotional needs, forming the basis for secure attachment. The consistent responsiveness of primary caregivers plays a pivotal role in shaping a child's sense of security and trust in relationships. Infants in securely attached relationships typically display a healthy balance between seeking comfort from their caregiver and exploring their surrounding environment. This phenomenon is often referred to as the 'secure base' effect, where the child uses the caregiver as a source of support while venturing out to explore their surroundings. Research indicates that secure infants are more likely to exhibit greater curiosity, self-reliance, and emotional regulation due to the trust and security established in their early interactions. Caregivers who are emotionally attuned and responsive to their child's signals help instill a sense of predictability and safety, reinforcing the child's confidence in exploring their environment. The quality of early relationships also shapes a child's ability to regulate emotions and cope with stress later in life. Moreover, secure attachments in early childhood contribute significantly to the development of positive self-esteem and empathy. These foundational interactions lay the groundwork for future relationships, influencing how individuals perceive and engage with others throughout their lives. Understanding the critical role of early childhood experiences in fostering secure attachments is fundamental for parents, educators, and professionals working with young children.

2. Secure Attachment During Adolescence - Key Indicators:

During adolescence, the manifestations of secure attachment play a pivotal role in shaping an individual's social and emotional development. Key indicators of secure attachment during this developmental stage include a strong sense of self-worth and autonomy, the ability to form meaningful and reciprocal relationships, and the capacity to effectively manage emotions and address conflicts. Adolescents with secure attachments tend to exhibit higher levels of resilience, self-confidence, and empathy, which contribute to their overall well-being and success in various social contexts. These individuals are more likely to seek out and maintain healthy peer relationships, communicate openly with peers and authority figures, and demonstrate adaptive coping strategies when faced with challenges. Furthermore, they are better equipped to explore their own identity, aspirations, and values, while simultaneously respecting the perspectives and boundaries of others. Securely attached adolescents also display greater academic motivation and achievement, as well as a reduced likelihood of engaging in risky behaviors such as substance abuse and delinquency. Additionally, they are more receptive to guidance and support from caregivers, teachers, and mentors, fostering a positive cycle of reinforcement for their secure attachment style. Recognizing the key indicators of secure attachment during adolescence is instrumental in promoting the healthy development of young individuals and equipping them with the necessary skills to thrive in their future interpersonal relationships and endeavors.

3. Adult Relationships - Manifestations of Security:

In adult relationships, the manifestations of security derived from a background of secure attachment during childhood are profound and far-reaching. Individuals with a secure attachment style typically exhibit several key behaviors and characteristics that contribute to healthy and fulfilling adult relationships. These individuals are more likely to display higher levels of empathy, emotional intelligence, and effective communication skills. Their ability to form strong, trusting connections allows for the development of stable and supportive partnerships, whether in romantic relationships, friendships, or professional collaborations. Securely attached adults are adept at managing conflict constructively, as they approach disagreements with a focus on mutual understanding and resolution rather than power struggles or avoidance. They demonstrate a willingness to be vulnerable and express their needs and feelings openly, fostering an environment of honesty and trust. Additionally, their secure base provides a source of comfort and assurance, enabling them to explore their emotions and experiences more freely within their relationships. Furthermore, individuals with secure attachments are more likely to seek out and maintain quality relationships due to their positive expectations and beliefs about themselves and others. This fundamental sense of security also translates into resilience when faced with challenges, allowing them to manage setbacks and uncertainties with the assurance that they are worthy of care and support.

4. Parenting Styles and Secure Attachments in Offspring:

Parenting styles play a crucial role in shaping the secure attachments that offspring develop throughout their lives. Research has consistently shown that the quality of early parental relationships significantly influences a child's ability to form secure attachments in subsequent relationships. In the context of secure attachment, parenting styles characterized by warmth, responsiveness, and consistent support have been found to be particularly impactful. Children raised by parents who demonstrate sensitive and nurturing behaviors tend to display higher levels of trust, empathy, and self-confidence, essential components of secure attachments. Conversely, authoritarian or neglectful parenting styles may hinder the development of secure attachments, leading to emotional insecurity and difficulties in forming healthy relationships. It is important to note that the impact of parenting styles on secure attachments extends beyond infancy and early childhood. Adolescents and young adults who experienced secure attachments during their formative years often exhibit greater autonomy, assertiveness, and resilience in managing interpersonal relationships. Moreover, the influence of secure parental attachments extends into adulthood, as individuals who had secure attachments with their caregivers tend to exhibit more positive and fulfilling relationships with their own partners and children. Recognizing the significance of parenting styles in fostering secure attachments can inform interventions and support programs aimed at promoting healthy family dynamics. By empowering parents with knowledge about the critical role they play in shaping their children's attachment patterns, professionals in the fields of psychology, education, and social work can help facilitate the development of secure and resilient individuals.

5. The Role of Secure Attachment in Workplace Dynamics:

In the contemporary professional landscape, the concept of secure attachment has garnered significant attention due to its potential impact on workplace dynamics. Individuals with secure attachment styles often exhibit noteworthy interpersonal skills and emotional regulation, which can significantly influence their interactions within organizational settings. One of the key aspects of secure attachment in the workplace is the ability to form healthy and productive relationships with colleagues and superiors. This is attributed to the individual's capacity to trust and connect with others, communicate effectively, and collaborate in team environments. Moreover, individuals with secure attachment demonstrate resilience and adaptability in the face of workplace challenges, contributing to a more positive work environment. Their confidence in seeking support and providing assistance also fosters a culture of mutual respect and cooperation. Furthermore, the emotional intelligence associated with secure attachment enhances an individual's capacity for conflict resolution and constructive feedback, thus promoting a harmonious and productive workplace atmosphere. Another crucial element is the impact of secure attachment on leadership qualities. Individuals with secure attachments are often perceived as empathetic, approachable, and trustworthy leaders. They are adept at motivating and inspiring their teams, creating a supportive and inclusive work environment. Additionally, their ability to manage stress and pressure while maintaining focus on long-term goals is instrumental in effective decision-making and problem-solving. Organizations benefit from nurturing a workforce with secure attachment styles as they contribute to higher employee engagement, lower turnover rates, and enhanced overall productivity. Recognizing the significance of secure attachment in workplace dynamics underscores the importance of cultivating a corporate culture that values emotional well-being and fosters strong interpersonal connections.

6. Coping Mechanisms in Secure Individuals:

Secure attachment individuals have developed coping mechanisms that enable them to manage life's challenges with a sense of resilience and adaptability. These individuals exhibit a remarkable capacity to manage stress and anxiety, displaying a balanced approach to dealing with difficult situations. One of the key coping mechanisms observed in secure individuals is emotional regulation. They possess the ability to identify and express their emotions in a healthy manner, thus avoiding the detrimental effects of repressed feelings. This emotional intelligence allows secure individuals to maintain a sense of equilibrium even in the face of adversity. Additionally, secure individuals often demonstrate strong problem-solving skills. Their ability to assess and address challenges pragmatically contributes to their overall psychological well-being. Furthermore, they exhibit a high level of self-efficacy, believing in their capability to overcome obstacles and achieve set goals. This confidence mitigates feelings of helplessness and fosters a solution-oriented mindset. Another crucial coping mechanism evident in secure individuals is the capacity for seeking social support. Having formed trusting relationships early in life, these individuals are adept at reaching out to others for assistance when needed. This network of supportive connections serves as a buffer against stress and promotes a sense of belonging and security. Moreover, secure individuals possess an optimistic outlook towards life, which acts as a protective factor in managing adversity. Their positive mindset enables them to reframe negative experiences and maintain hope for the future. Additionally, secure individuals tend to engage in adaptive coping strategies such as seeking out leisure activities, engaging in physical exercise, and practicing mindfulness and relaxation techniques. These proactive approaches contribute to their overall mental and physical well-being. Lastly, secure individuals often exhibit a strong sense of identity and purpose, which provides them with a solid foundation during times of distress. Their clarity of goals and values serves as a guiding force, offering a sense of direction and meaning amidst challenging circumstances. Overall, the coping mechanisms displayed by secure individuals exemplify their capacity for emotional maturity, resilience, and the ability to thrive in various aspects of life.

7. Impact on Mental and Physical Health:

Research has indicated that individuals with secure attachments tend to exhibit lower levels of anxiety, depression, and psychological distress. Additionally, they are more likely to display higher levels of self-esteem and overall well-being. This emotional stability is attributed to the consistent support and responsiveness experienced in their early relationships, which lays the foundation for a healthy sense of self-worth and confidence in managing life's challenges. Moreover, the physiological benefits of secure attachment cannot be overlooked. Studies have shown that adults with secure attachments tend to have stronger immune systems, reduced cardiovascular reactivity to stress, and better overall physical health. The sense of security instilled by early attachment experiences fosters a neural regulatory system, contributing to a more adaptive stress response and resilience against the negative effects of chronic stress. Beyond the individual level, the impact of secure attachment on mental and physical health extends to interpersonal relationships and societal dynamics. Securely attached individuals are more adept at forming and maintaining fulfilling relationships, as they possess the ability to manage conflicts constructively and express empathy towards others. This not only enriches their personal lives but also contributes to a more harmonious and supportive social environment. Furthermore, the collective presence of securely attached individuals in communities can foster a positive cycle of emotional well-being and resilience, helping to mitigate the impact of societal stressors and adversities.

8. Long-Term Benefits:

Emotional and social competence are fundamental aspects of human development that are significantly influenced by attachment styles, particularly secure attachments. Research has shown that individuals with a history of secure attachments throughout their lifespan often exhibit enhanced emotional regulation skills and greater social competence compared to those with insecure attachment patterns. These long-term benefits can be observed across various domains of life, including personal relationships, academic or professional success, and overall well-being. Understanding the specific ways in which secure attachments contribute to emotional and social competence is essential for comprehending the profound impact of attachment theory on human development.

In the area of emotional competence, individuals with a secure attachment history tend to display a strong capacity to recognize, comprehend, and express their emotions effectively. This heightened emotional awareness enables them to manage challenging situations with resilience and adaptability, as they are more adept at managing stress, anxiety, and other negative emotions. Moreover, secure individuals often demonstrate a greater propensity for empathy and compassion towards others, fostering healthier interpersonal connections and contributing to a supportive social environment.

The influence of secure attachments on social competence becomes evident through the establishment of trusting and fulfilling relationships. As individuals with secure attachment styles have experienced consistent and reliable caregiving in their formative years, they tend to develop a positive internal working model of relationships, leading to increased confidence in forming and maintaining healthy attachments. Securely attached individuals are more likely to engage in constructive communication, assertiveness, and cooperation within their social interactions, thereby cultivating harmonious and resilient relationships with peers, partners, and colleagues.

The effects of emotional and social competence stemming from secure attachments extend into adulthood and significantly impact various facets of life. For instance, individuals with secure attachment orientations often exhibit higher levels of self-esteem, optimism, and overall psychological well-being, which can bolster their resilience in the face of adversity and aid in the pursuit of personal and professional goals. Additionally, the capacity to form secure attachments in adulthood, based on early experiences, contributes to a sense of fulfillment and satisfaction in intimate relationships, offering a protective factor against mental health challenges and enhancing overall life satisfaction.

Anxious Attachment - Origins, Development, and Traits

1. Definition:

Anxious attachment is a complex emotional and psychological condition marked by a profound fear of abandonment and an overwhelming desire for emotional closeness in relationships. Individuals experiencing anxious attachment often find themselves plagued by constant worry about the stability of their relationships and the fear of being left alone. This fear is deeply ingrained and can significantly impact the individual's overall well-being and interpersonal interactions. The origins of anxious attachment can be traced back to early childhood experiences, particularly within the context of the parent-child relationship. This formative period plays a crucial role in shaping the individual's attachment style and laying the groundwork for their future emotional connections. It is important to note that anxious attachment is not a uniform experience and can manifest differently from one individual to another. Notably, individuals with anxious attachment tendencies may display behaviors such as seeking excessive reassurance, exhibiting jealousy or clinginess, and experiencing heightened anxiety when separated from their partners. These behaviors are driven by an intense need for emotional validation and security, often rooted in past experiences that have left emotional scars. Additionally, the tendency towards anxious attachment is often intertwined with underlying feelings of inadequacy, low self-esteem, and a consistent yearning for acceptance and approval.

2. Historical Perspectives and Theoretical Underpinnings:

The understanding of anxious attachment has evolved significantly over time. John Bowlby's groundbreaking work emphasized the profound impact of early maternal separation on an infant's emotional development, formulating the basis for the concept of attachment. Mary Ainsworth then further expanded Bowlby's theory through her renowned 'Strange Situation' experiments, which classified attachment patterns into secure, anxious-ambivalent, and avoidant categories.

On the other hand, the influence of psychoanalytic thought, particularly the works of Sigmund Freud and Erik Erikson, has left an indelible mark on the understanding of anxious attachment. Freud's emphasis on the significance of early caregiver-child interactions and the formation of the superego profoundly influenced subsequent attachment research. Similarly, Erikson's psychosocial stages of development shed light on the pivotal role of trust versus mistrust during infancy, elucidating the developmental underpinnings of anxious attachment patterns.

As attachment theory continued to evolve, contemporary perspectives from various disciplines, including developmental psychology, neuroscience, and social work, have enriched our understanding of anxious attachment. The integration of evolutionary psychology has provided valuable insights into the adaptive function of attachment behaviors in human evolution, shedding light on the roots of anxious attachment in ancestral caregiving dynamics and environmental pressures. Additionally, cognitive theories have elucidated the role of internal working models and mental representations in shaping anxious attachment, offering a comprehensive framework to comprehend the cognitive-affective components of attachment processes.

Lastly, the ecological systems perspective, championed by Urie Bronfenbrenner, highlighted the multifaceted influences of family, community, and culture on the development of attachment patterns, underscoring the complex interplay between individual temperament and environmental influences.

3. Early Childhood Experiences and Environmental Factors:

During childhood, children form their first relationships with primary caregivers, which lay the foundation for future interpersonal interactions and emotional regulation. The quality of these early experiences and the environmental factors surrounding the child significantly impact the emergence of anxious attachment patterns.

The caregiving environment, including the responsiveness, consistency, and sensitivity of caregivers, greatly influences the child's sense of security and trust. Infants and young children who experience inconsistent or inadequate caregiving may develop heightened distress and preoccupation with maintaining proximity to their caregivers, leading to the manifestation of anxious attachment. Additionally, exposure to prolonged periods of parental stress, marital conflict, or disruptions in caregiving due to external factors can contribute to the development of anxious attachment tendencies.

The broader social and cultural context in which a child is raised can shape their attachment experiences. Societal norms, community support systems, and economic conditions all impact the availability of resources and support for families, influencing the stability and predictability of the child's environment. A lack of social support or exposure to adverse socioeconomic conditions can heighten the risk of developing anxious attachment, as it may compromise the ability of caregivers to provide consistent and responsive care.

Traumatic experiences, such as abuse, neglect, or separations from caregivers, can significantly disrupt the attachment formation process, leading to elevated anxiety and fear of abandonment in the child. These early adversities can leave a lasting impact on the child's psychological well-being and their capacity to establish secure and trusting relationships in the future.

4. The Role of Parenting Styles in the Formation of Anxious Attachments:

Parenting styles significantly influence the development of attachment patterns in children, particularly in the formation of anxious attachments. Authoritative parenting, characterized by warmth, responsiveness, and clear boundaries, tends to foster secure attachments, while authoritarian and permissive parenting styles are more closely associated with the development of anxious attachment patterns. Authoritarian parents often exhibit high levels of control and low emotional responsiveness, leading children to develop anxiety and a sense of insecurity in their relationships. On the other hand, permissive parenting, marked by indulgence and low demands on children, can result in inconsistent caregiving and lack of structure, contributing to the development of attachment-related anxiety. Understanding how different parenting styles impact attachment formation is crucial for recognizing early signs of anxious attachment in children and providing appropriate interventions. The delicate balance between warmth and structure in parenting is essential for nurturing secure attachments and promoting emotional well-being.

5. Neurobiological Correlates:

The formation of anxious attachments is closely linked to neurobiological processes that influence brain development. Understanding the neurobiological correlates of anxious attachment provides a critical framework for comprehending the underlying mechanisms involved in the manifestation of this attachment style. Neuroscientific research has demonstrated that early experiences and environmental factors play a pivotal role in shaping the structural and functional development of the brain, particularly in regions associated with emotional regulation and stress responsiveness. These experiences have a profound impact on the architecture of the developing brain, leading to lasting effects on an individual's emotional well-being and interpersonal relationships. The interplay between genetic predispositions and early life experiences further contributes to the neurobiological underpinnings of anxious attachment. Studies have highlighted the significance of neurotransmitters such as serotonin and oxytocin in modulating attachment-related behaviors and affective responses. Dysregulation of these neurochemical systems can contribute to heightened emotional reactivity and difficulty in managing stress, characteristic features of anxious attachment. Moreover, advances in neuroimaging techniques have provided insights into the neural circuits involved in processing social cues and regulating attachment-related emotions. Functional magnetic resonance imaging (fMRI) studies have revealed aberrant activation patterns in brain regions such as the amygdala, prefrontal cortex, and insula among individuals with anxious attachment, suggesting altered neural processing of emotional stimuli and interpersonal interactions. Additionally, neuroplasticity, the brain's capacity to adapt and reorganize in response to experiences, offers hope for intervention and therapeutic interventions aimed at promoting secure attachment. Understanding the neurobiological foundations of anxious attachment not only sheds light on the etiology of this attachment style but also underscores the need for holistic approaches that integrate psychological, biological, and social dimensions in addressing attachment-related challenges.

6. Developmental Trajectories - Infancy Through Adolescence:

The developmental trajectories of anxious attachment from infancy through adolescence are marked by various nuanced patterns of behavior and emotional responses. During infancy, the key developmental milestone is the establishment of a secure base with the primary caregiver. However, infants with anxious attachment may exhibit heightened distress upon separation from their caregivers and display ambivalent behaviors upon reunion. These early experiences lay the foundation for subsequent developmental pathways. As these children transition into early childhood, their anxious attachment may manifest in seeking excessive reassurance, exhibiting clingy behaviors, and struggling with emotional regulation. Their developing cognitive abilities enable them to form internal working models of relationships, leading to a pervasive sense of insecurity and fears of abandonment. Throughout middle childhood, anxious attachment can surface in the form of heightened dependence on parental figures, an increased fear of rejection, and difficulties establishing healthy peer relationships. As these individuals manage the challenges of adolescence, their anxious attachment may contribute to an amplified fear of intimacy, persistent self-doubt, and a tendency to engage in preoccupied thoughts about relationships. Furthermore, the hormonal changes and social pressures characteristic of this developmental stage can exacerbate existing attachment-related anxieties. Consequently, adolescents with anxious attachment may grapple with conflicting desires for connection and avoidance, leading to complex relationship dynamics. The interplay between biological maturation, environmental influences, and attachment experiences shapes the developmental trajectories of individuals with anxious attachment, influencing their emotional well-being and interpersonal connections as they progress through different life stages.

7. Adult Manifestations of Anxious Attachment:

In adulthood, the manifestations of anxious attachment can significantly impact various aspects of an individual's life. Adults with anxious attachment tendencies often demonstrate a heightened need for reassurance and validation in their relationships. They may exhibit behaviors such as excessive seeking of closeness, a fear of abandonment, and heightened sensitivity to perceived threats of rejection or disconnection. These individuals tend to rely heavily on their partners for emotional support and frequently seek proximity to avoid feelings of insecurity or loneliness. As a result, they may struggle with establishing healthy boundaries and autonomy within their relationships. Additionally, adults with anxious attachment patterns may experience intense emotional responses to relationship stressors, leading to difficulties in regulating their emotions and managing interpersonal conflicts effectively. Their fear of rejection and abandonment can also manifest in a constant desire for closeness, which may become overwhelming for their partners. This can lead to cycles of push-pull behavior, where the individual vacillates between seeking proximity and feeling overwhelmed by intimacy, creating instability in their relationships. Furthermore, adults with anxious attachment tendencies may exhibit self-critical and self-doubting thoughts, constantly questioning their self-worth and desirability, which can undermine their confidence and overall well-being. Consequently, this may contribute to a persistent sense of dissatisfaction and emotional distress in their relationships. It is crucial to recognize that these manifestations are not indicative of personal flaws but rather the long-lasting impact of early attachment experiences. Understanding the adult manifestations of anxious attachment is essential for clinicians, therapists, and individuals themselves to recognize and address these patterns effectively. By gaining insight into these manifestations, individuals can begin to develop healthier relational dynamics, improve emotional regulation, and foster greater security in their intimate connections. Acknowledging these manifestations and their underlying causes can serve as a catalyst for personal growth, healing, and the cultivation of more secure attachments in adulthood.

8. Common Psychological and Emotional Traits:

The manifestations of anxious attachment in adulthood are often characterized by a range of psychological and emotional traits that significantly impact an individual's daily experiences and relationships. One common trait observed in individuals with anxious attachment is heightened sensitivity to perceived cues of rejection or abandonment. This hypersensitivity can lead to a pervasive fear of being left or unloved, which may result in overreacting to minor relationship issues and seeking excessive reassurance from partners or loved ones.

Additionally, individuals with anxious attachment often exhibit tendencies toward excessive worrying and rumination about their relationships. They may engage in repetitive and intrusive thoughts regarding the stability and security of their attachments, leading to significant emotional distress and impaired functioning. This relentless preoccupation can also contribute to feelings of inadequacy and self-doubt, impacting their overall well-being.

As a result of their underlying fear of abandonment, individuals with anxious attachment may display a propensity for clingy or dependent behavior within their relationships. This behavior may stem from a deep-seated desire for closeness and validation, yet it can also inadvertently push partners away and create further turmoil in the relationship dynamics.

It is not uncommon for individuals with anxious attachment to experience difficulties in regulating their emotions, particularly when confronted with perceived threats to their attachments. Heightened levels of anxiety, insecurity, and emotional reactivity are frequently reported, leading to challenges in effectively managing interpersonal conflicts and stressors. These emotional fluctuations can significantly impact the individual's ability to maintain stable and fulfilling relationships, contributing to recurrent patterns of relational turmoil.

In addition to these psychological and emotional traits, individuals with anxious attachment may also demonstrate a tendency to idealize their partners as a means of quelling their fears of abandonment. This idealization can lead to unrealistic expectations and a heightened vulnerability to disappointment, as the discrepancy between fantasy and reality becomes apparent. Consequently, the ongoing struggle to reconcile these idealized perceptions with the complexities of real-life relationships adds another layer of strain to their emotional well-being.

9. Influence of Societal and Cultural Contexts:

The influence of societal and cultural contexts on attachment styles is a subject of profound significance, with far-reaching implications for our understanding of human relationships. Societal norms and cultural practices play a pivotal role in shaping individual attachment patterns from early childhood through adulthood. In many societies, the prevailing cultural values, traditions, and family structures directly impact the development and expression of attachment styles. Cultural attitudes towards emotional expression, autonomy, and interdependence can significantly influence the formation and maintenance of attachment bonds. Moreover, societal expectations regarding gender roles, familial obligations, and social hierarchy can subtly shape the attachment dynamics within interpersonal relationships.

Cultural diversity also contributes to the variances in attachment styles observed across different populations. The ways in which attachment behaviors are perceived, interpreted, and responded to may vary drastically among distinct cultural groups. For instance, collectivist cultures often prioritize group harmony and interdependency, which can foster attachment patterns emphasizing interconnectedness and harmonious social integration. Contrastingly, individualistic cultures may endorse self-reliance and personal autonomy, potentially leading to attachment tendencies characterized by independence and self-sufficiency. These diverse cultural frameworks inevitably leave an indelible imprint on the formation and expression of attachment styles within specific communities.

The impact of globalization and acculturation processes cannot be overlooked when examining the influence of societal and cultural contexts on attachment. As individuals traverse multicultural environments and cope with diverse value systems, their attachment orientations may undergo adaptation or modification. The interplay between one's original cultural background and the norms of the host society can yield unique amalgamations of attachment styles, influencing the complexities of interpersonal relationships.

Impact of Anxious Attachment on Interpersonal Relationships

1. Emotional Dependencies and Anxiety Manifestations:

Emotional dependency is a recurring theme in anxious attachment, characterized by an intense reliance on the partner for emotional validation, reassurance, and a sense of security. Individuals with anxious attachment may exhibit behaviors such as seeking constant contact and reassurance from their partners, experiencing heightened sensitivity to perceived rejection or abandonment, and struggling with self-soothing capabilities when faced with relationship challenges. This reliance can lead to a cycle of insecurity and heightened anxiety within the relationship, often contributing to a pattern of emotional turbulence and distress.

Anxiety manifestations in relationships associated with anxious attachment often manifest through amplified emotional reactions and an overarching fear of rejection or loss. Individuals may find themselves oscillating between periods of intense longing for closeness and the overwhelming fear of being left alone. These manifestations can create a challenging dynamic, impacting communication patterns, conflict resolution, and overall relationship satisfaction. The palpable presence of anxiety within these relationships can lead to a pervasive sense of unease, hindering the establishment of a secure and harmonious connection.

The emotional dependencies and anxiety manifestations associated with anxious attachment can also influence individuals' perceptions of self-worth and competence within the context of their relationships. These individuals may harbor deep-seated doubts about their own value, fearing that their needs and emotions are burdensome to their partners. As a result, they may struggle to express their feelings openly, resulting in a suppressed emotional state and further exacerbating their internalized anxiety.

2. Communication Patterns and Conflict Resolution:

Communication patterns and conflict resolution are critical elements in understanding the impact of anxious attachment on interpersonal relationships. Individuals with anxious attachment often exhibit unique communication styles characterized by heightened emotional reactivity, fear of abandonment, and a deep-seated need for reassurance. These patterns can significantly influence how conflicts are approached and resolved within relationships.

Anxious individuals may struggle with assertive communication, often engaging in passive or aggressive behaviors due to their underlying fears and insecurities. This can lead to challenges in openly expressing needs, setting boundaries, or addressing concerns, all of which are essential components of healthy communication. Furthermore, the heightened emotional reactivity inherent in anxious attachment can amplify conflicts, making it challenging to engage in constructive dialogue without escalating tension.

Conflict resolution within relationships involving anxious attachment requires a thoughtful and empathetic approach. Partners and individuals close to those with anxious attachment must demonstrate patience, active listening, and validation of emotions to manage these situations effectively. Addressing the root causes of distress and anxiety can help de-escalate conflicts and foster healthier communication dynamics.

Therapeutic interventions focused on improving communication and conflict resolution skills can be valuable for individuals with anxious attachment, offering them tools to express themselves more effectively and manage conflicts in a constructive manner. Providing strategies for effective communication, such as active listening techniques, non-violent communication methods, and conflict de-escalation approaches, can empower individuals to address interpersonal challenges with greater confidence and resilience.

It's important for both partners in a relationship involving anxious attachment to recognize the potential impact of communication patterns and conflict resolution on the overall health of their connection. By fostering an environment of open communication, mutual respect, and empathy, partners can work together to address conflicts and strengthen their bond. Recognizing and acknowledging each other's attachment needs and adjusting communication styles accordingly can contribute to a more secure and fulfilling relationship.

3. Impact on Romantic Partnerships:

Anxious attachment can significantly impact romantic partnerships, often influencing the dynamics and overall health of the relationship. Individuals with anxious attachment styles may exhibit a heightened need for reassurance and validation from their partners, leading to an increased dependence on their romantic relationships as a primary source of security and self-worth. This reliance on external validation can manifest in behaviors such as seeking constant communication, expressing fears of abandonment, and experiencing heightened levels of jealousy and insecurity.

The tendency to overanalyze interactions, coupled with a fear of rejection, can lead individuals with anxious attachment to interpret ambiguous cues as indicators of potential abandonment or disinterest from their partners. As a result, they might engage in preemptive measures to maintain closeness and avoid feelings of abandonment, which can sometimes inadvertently create tension or pressure within the relationship.

In romantic partnerships, the impact of anxious attachment can be observed in various aspects of the relationship, including intimacy, communication, and overall satisfaction. The persistent need for reassurance and fears of rejection can influence an individual's approach to intimacy, potentially leading to a reliance on the partner to fulfill emotional needs and provide a sense of security. This dependency can affect the balance of give-and-take in the relationship, potentially creating strain and compromising individual autonomy.

Communication in romantic partnerships involving an anxious attachment style may also be affected. Individuals with anxious attachment may struggle with effectively expressing their needs and concerns, often due to underlying fears of rejection or conflict. This can result in patterns of hyper-vigilance, where minor fluctuations in the partner's behavior are closely monitored, and any perceived deviation from expected responses may trigger heightened anxiety or distress.

Additionally, within romantic partnerships, the impact of anxious attachment on conflict resolution strategies cannot be overlooked. Individuals with anxious attachment may display tendencies to avoid or overly accommodate during conflicts, driven by a fear of jeopardizing the relationship. This can lead to difficulties in addressing and resolving differences, potentially contributing to recurring conflicts or unmet needs within the relationship.

4. Influence on Friendships and Social Circles:

An individual's anxious attachment style can significantly impact their ability to form and sustain healthy friendships and social interactions. The underlying fear of abandonment and intense desire for closeness inherent in anxious attachment can manifest in various ways, influencing the dynamics of friendships and social circles. One key aspect affected by anxious attachment is the tendency to seek excessive reassurance and validation from friends, leading to potential strains in these relationships. Individuals with an anxious attachment style may demonstrate clingy behavior or become overly sensitive to perceived threats of rejection, thereby creating a challenging dynamic within their social circles. Additionally, the fear of being abandoned or unloved may prompt individuals with anxious attachment to exhibit possessive or controlling behaviors, potentially driving their friends away. These manifestations can hinder the formation of balanced and reciprocal friendships, as they may create imbalances in terms of emotional labor and foster codependent patterns. Furthermore, the high sensitivity to interpersonal cues commonly observed in individuals with anxious attachment can lead to misinterpretations of social signals, resulting in heightened levels of jealousy, insecurity, and mistrust within friendships. Consequently, these negative thought patterns and behaviors may contribute to strained social circles and limited social support networks for individuals with anxious attachment. Building awareness around the influence of anxious attachment on friendships and social circles is crucial for fostering healthier and more fulfilling social connections. By recognizing the impact of their attachment style, individuals can actively work towards developing strategies to mitigate the negative effects on their friendships. Engaging in open and honest communication with friends about their attachment-related concerns and seeking professional guidance can aid in managing the complexities of forming and maintaining supportive peer relationships. Moreover, cultivating self-awareness and practicing self-soothing techniques can empower individuals with anxious attachment to manage their emotions and expectations within their social circles. Embracing mindfulness and introspection can also help individuals identify and challenge maladaptive thought patterns, allowing for a more balanced and harmonious approach to engaging with friends.

5. Parental Influences and Family Dynamics:

In the framework of attachment theory, the influence of parental relationships and family dynamics holds profound significance in shaping an individual's attachment style, particularly in the context of anxious attachment. Anxious attachment often derives from early experiences within the family unit, where caregivers may have displayed inconsistent responsiveness or emotional availability, leading the individual to develop a heightened need for validation and reassurance in subsequent relationships. Understanding the impact of parental influences and family dynamics on anxious attachment requires a comprehensive exploration of multiple factors.

Firstly, the quality of attachment between the individual and their primary caregivers lays the foundation for understanding anxious attachment. Caregivers who demonstrate inconsistent or unpredictable responses to a child's distress signals can contribute to the development of an anxious attachment style, as the child learns to hypermonitor the caregiver's availability in times of need. This tendency to seek proximity and reassurance can perpetuate into adult relationships, impacting the individual's ability to trust and effectively regulate their emotions within interpersonal connections.

On the other hand, family dynamics play a pivotal role in shaping an individual's attachment style. The presence of conflict, unresolved issues, or systemic dysfunction within the family environment can contribute to an atmosphere of emotional insecurity, thereby reinforcing patterns of anxious attachment. As individuals manage familial interactions characterized by tension or unpredictability, they may internalize a constant need for external validation and struggle with developing a secure sense of self-worth.

Additionally, exploring the intergenerational transmission of attachment patterns within families offers valuable insights into the perpetuation of anxious attachment across generations.

Individuals raised by parents with anxious attachment tendencies may themselves be at an increased risk of developing similar relational patterns, thus highlighting the cyclical nature of attachment dynamics within family systems.

The role of parental figures in providing models for healthy emotional regulation and interpersonal behavior cannot be overstated. Caregivers who demonstrate secure attachment traits through consistent support, empathy, and effective communication can mitigate the risk of anxious attachment in their children, fostering a stable foundation for the development of secure relationship patterns.

6. Therapeutic Approaches and Interventions:

Therapeutic interventions for addressing anxious attachment in interpersonal relationships are vital for facilitating positive change and personal growth. Firstly, cognitive-behavioral therapy (CBT) stands as one of the most widely used and effective modalities for addressing anxious attachment. By identifying and restructuring maladaptive thought patterns and behaviors, CBT aims to alleviate anxiety and enhance self-esteem and relational skills. Additionally, mindfulness-based interventions have gained prominence in recent years for their ability to cultivate self-awareness, emotional regulation, and compassionate acceptance, thus directly targeting the underlying mechanisms of anxious attachment. Moreover, attachment-focused therapies, such as Emotionally Focused Therapy (EFT), aim to restructure attachment bonds and foster secure connections within relationships by addressing core emotional needs and fears. Another essential aspect is the inclusion of psychoeducation, which equips individuals with a deeper understanding of attachment dynamics, empowering them to recognize and modify detrimental relationship patterns. Furthermore, interpersonal therapy provides a supportive, non-judgmental space for individuals to explore and address relational difficulties through collaborative problem-solving and communication enhancement. Beyond these therapeutic modalities, the exploration of narrative and schema therapies can aid individuals in reframing their relationship narratives and reconstructing core beliefs, ultimately promoting healthier perspectives and interactions. It is imperative for clinicians to tailor interventions to fit the unique cultural background and specific needs of each individual, acknowledging the potential influence of cultural factors on attachment styles and relationship dynamics.

7. Long-term Implications for Relationship Development:

Establishing a clear understanding of the long-term implications of anxious attachment on relationship development is crucial in comprehending its pervasive influence. Over time, individuals with anxious attachment may experience challenges in sustaining healthy and fulfilling relationships, as their underlying fears and insecurities often manifest in various detrimental ways. It becomes evident that the impact of anxious attachment extends far beyond the initial stages of a relationship and can significantly shape the course of long-term interpersonal dynamics.

When examining the long-term implications, it is imperative to acknowledge the potential erosion of trust and emotional stability within relationships. Individuals with anxious attachment tendencies may struggle with ongoing feelings of insecurity and doubt, leading to difficulties in maintaining a sense of security and closeness with their partners. This persistent unease can create recurring cycles of emotional turmoil and strain, hindering the establishment of enduring, harmonious connections.

The long-term repercussions of anxious attachment can be observed in the sphere of personal growth and fulfillment within relationships. As individuals manage the complexities of intimate connections, their anxious predispositions may impede the cultivation of independence and self-assurance. This can foster an overreliance on the validation and reassurance from their partners, potentially stifling mutual growth and autonomy within the relationship.

In addition, the effects of anxious attachment on relationship development are underscored by the profound impact on conflict resolution and communication patterns. Over time, individuals may find themselves caught in repetitive cycles of maladaptive communication and heightened emotional reactivity, impeding the resolution of relationship conflicts and fostering emotional distance. These entrenched patterns can ultimately impede the development of resilient and adaptive communication strategies, thereby perpetuating relational challenges.

The long-term implications extend to the broader implications for overall well-being and mental health. Prolonged experiences of anxiety and insecurity within relationships can contribute to heightened stress levels and emotional dysregulation, potentially impacting one's psychological resilience and overall emotional well-being. Consequently, these enduring implications emphasize the critical importance of addressing and understanding anxious attachment within the context of long-term relationship development.

Dynamics of Avoidant Attachment

1. Psychosocial Underpinnings of Avoidance Behaviors:

Avoidant attachment behaviors often stem from a complex interplay of psychosocial factors that shape an individual's relational patterns and coping mechanisms. It is crucial to understand that avoidant attachment is not merely a solitary trait but rather a manifestation of multifaceted influences encompassing early experiences, familial dynamics, and social interactions. One of the key psychosocial factors influencing avoidance behaviors is the quality of early caregiver relationships. Research suggests that inconsistent or emotionally unavailable caregiving during infancy and early childhood can set the stage for the emergence of avoidant attachment patterns. Children who experience caregivers as unpredictable or unresponsive may internalize a sense of self-reliance and emotional suppression as adaptive strategies to cope with their unmet attachment needs. Furthermore, familial dynamics, such as parental divorce, family conflict, or parental mental health issues, can significantly contribute to the development of avoidant attachment tendencies. Additionally, societal norms and cultural values play a pivotal role in shaping individuals' attachment orientations. Societies that emphasize independence, emotional restraint, and self-sufficiency may inadvertently foster an environment conducive to the cultivation of avoidant attachment tendencies. Moreover, experiences of rejection, bullying, or social exclusion during formative years can fuel the adoption of avoidant coping mechanisms as a protective shield against perceived threats to emotional vulnerability. Moreover, the impact of psychosocial stressors, including trauma, loss, and adverse life events, cannot be undermined in understanding the genesis of avoidance behaviors within attachment dynamics. These stressors can engender a heightened hypervigilance towards potential relational threats, leading individuals to adopt avoidant strategies as a means of self-preservation.

2. Neurobiological Perspectives on Avoidant Attachment:

From the perspective of neuroscience, the regulation of emotional responses and social bonding is a product of the interplay between the limbic system and prefrontal cortex. Individuals exhibiting avoidant attachment tendencies often display distinct patterns in these neural circuits that impact their ability to form and maintain intimate relationships. Research has indicated that the amygdala, a key structure responsible for processing emotions, shows heightened activity among individuals with avoidant attachment, particularly when encountering emotional stimuli or perceived threats to autonomy and independence. Conversely, diminished activation in brain regions associated with social cognition, such as the ventral striatum and anterior cingulate cortex, is observed, suggesting reduced reward response and empathy toward others' emotions. Furthermore, neurochemical factors, including variations in oxytocin and vasopressin receptors, play a pivotal role in shaping attachment behaviors, particularly in the context of forming and maintaining close bonds. These biological substrates contribute to the characteristic emotional aloofness and self-reliance exhibited by individuals with avoidant attachment styles. Beyond the functional neuroanatomy, epigenetic mechanisms involving gene expression and hormonal regulation have also emerged as crucial elements influencing the formation of avoidant attachment patterns. Understanding the interplay between genetics, neurobiology, and environmental influences illuminates the complex etiology of avoidant attachment and paves the way for more tailored interventions aimed at addressing the underlying neurobiological mechanisms.

3. Developmental Pathways Leading to Avoidance:

Developmental pathways leading to avoidance behaviors in attachment can be traced back to early experiences and relationships during childhood. Research suggests that these pathways are influenced by various factors, including but not limited to caregivers' responsiveness, temperament, and environmental stressors. During the critical developmental period in early childhood, the quality of attachment relationships with primary caregivers plays a pivotal role in shaping an individual's attachment style. Children who experience inconsistent or unresponsive caregiving may develop adaptive strategies aimed at self-protection, leading to the formation of avoidant attachment patterns.

The temperament of the child can also play a significant role in the development of avoidant attachment. Some children may have an inherent predisposition towards heightened reactivity to stress or novelty, which can contribute to the adoption of avoidant coping mechanisms as a means of regulating their emotional experiences. These early experiences and individual characteristics interact with environmental stressors, such as family dynamics, socioeconomic challenges, or traumatic events, further shaping the developmental pathways towards avoidance.

The impact of parental modeling on the formation of avoidance cannot be understated. Children often learn and internalize attachment-related behaviors by observing and interacting with their primary caregivers. If a caregiver exhibits dismissive or emotionally distant behaviors, children may internalize these patterns and adopt similar strategies to cope with their own attachment needs. This process of social learning can establish enduring patterns of avoidance that persist into adulthood.

4. Cognitive and Emotional Patterns Characteristic of Avoidance:

Avoidant attachment is accompanied by distinct cognitive and emotional patterns that shape an individual's perception and interaction within relationships. Cognitively, individuals with avoidant attachment may exhibit a tendency to minimize the importance of attachment-related emotions and needs. This often manifests as a reluctance to acknowledge or express vulnerabilities and a preference for self-reliance. Such cognitive patterns are rooted in a defense mechanism against perceived threats to emotional autonomy and independence, leading the individual to prioritize detachment and emotional distance as a means of self-protection. Emotionally, individuals with avoidant attachment may experience difficulty in forming close emotional bonds and struggle with intimacy. This emotional pattern is underpinned by a fear of dependency and a heightened sensitivity to feelings of suffocation or engulfment within close relationships. As a result, individuals with avoidant attachment may employ strategies such as emotional distancing, compartmentalization of feelings, and a tendency to suppress or dismiss emotions as a means of coping. These cognitive and emotional patterns not only influence the individual's internal world but also have profound implications for their external interpersonal dynamics. It is crucial to recognize that these patterns are adaptive responses developed in early attachment experiences and continue to exert influence across the lifespan.

5. Behavioral Expressions of Avoidant Attachment in Relationships:

Individuals with avoidant attachment tendencies often exhibit distinct behavioral patterns within their relationships, stemming from their deeply ingrained fear of intimacy and reliance on self-reliance. When confronted with emotional closeness, avoidantly attached individuals may demonstrate a tendency to withdraw or create emotional distance as a mechanism to protect themselves from the potential vulnerabilities associated with intimate connections. This withdrawal can manifest through behaviors such as avoiding deep emotional conversations, deflecting expressions of affection, or exhibiting reluctance towards forming close bonds. Additionally, individuals with avoidant attachment may display an inclination towards maintaining a sense of independence by actively resisting dependency on their partners, preferring autonomy and individual pursuits over shared activities or obligations.

In romantic relationships, these individuals may struggle to fully invest themselves emotionally or commit to long-term intimacy, leading to a pattern of short-lived or tumultuous partnerships. Such relational dynamics can create significant challenges for their partners, often leaving them feeling unfulfilled, neglected, or rejected due to the avoidant individual's emotional unavailability. Furthermore, the avoidant partner's hesitation to express vulnerability or engage in open communication can lead to misunderstandings and misinterpretations, contributing to escalating tensions and conflicts within the relationship. As a result, the relational landscape for an avoidantly attached individual is often characterized by a cycle of distancing behaviors, intermittent displays of emotional detachment, and an apparent reluctance to nurture deep emotional connections.

Beyond romantic relationships, the impact of avoidant attachment extends to familial and social interactions, wherein individuals may struggle to establish and maintain meaningful connections. This could be evidenced by a preference for solitude, a tendency to prioritize self-reliance, and a reluctance to seek support or emotional validation from others. Whether in friendships, familial bonds, or professional environments, these behavioral expressions of avoidance can hinder the development of secure and nurturing relationships, resulting in feelings of isolation and detachment for both the individual and their counterparts.

6. Comparison with Other Attachment Styles:

When examining the dynamics of avoidant attachment, it is essential to conduct a comparative analysis with other attachment styles for a comprehensive understanding. One prominent contrast can be drawn between avoidant attachment and secure attachment. While secure individuals exhibit trust, comfort with intimacy, and effective communication in their relationships, individuals with avoidant attachment tend to display reluctance in forming close connections, fear of dependence, and a tendency to maintain emotional distance. This comparison highlights the stark differences in relational patterns and emotional regulation between these two attachment styles.

Another crucial comparison can be made with anxious attachment. Unlike avoidant individuals, those with anxious attachment often exhibit heightened emotional reactivity, constant need for reassurance, and fear of abandonment. This contrast illuminates the dissimilar coping strategies and emotional needs of individuals with anxious and avoidant attachment styles. Furthermore, exploring the similarities and differences in the behavioral expressions of avoidant and anxious attachment provides valuable insights into the underlying mechanisms that drive these distinct attachment patterns.

Additionally, a comparative analysis with disorganized attachment reveals intriguing nuances in relational behaviors. Disorganized attachment is characterized by unresolved trauma and inconsistency in approach to relationships. When juxtaposed with avoidant attachment, which is marked by emotional withdrawal and self-sufficiency, this examination sheds light on how differing experiences and coping mechanisms contribute to divergent attachment styles.

Comparing avoidant attachment with ambivalent attachment, also known as preoccupied attachment, elucidates the contrasting approaches to closeness and emotional connection. While ambivalent individuals may seek continuous validation and closeness in relationships, avoidant individuals often strive for independence and emotional autonomy. By examining these disparities, one gains a deeper appreciation of the variance in relational needs and interpersonal behaviors among individuals with different attachment styles.

7. Therapeutic Approaches to Addressing Avoidant Attachment:

Therapeutic interventions for addressing avoidant attachment necessitate a comprehensive and nuanced approach that acknowledges the unique challenges and complexities inherent in this attachment style. Therapists working with individuals presenting with avoidant attachment patterns must adopt an empathetic and patient-centered approach, recognizing the deep-seated fears and coping mechanisms characteristic of avoidant individuals.

One of the primary therapeutic strategies involves creating a secure and non-judgmental space in which the individual feels safe to explore and articulate their innermost thoughts, emotions, and relational patterns. This process often entails building a trusting therapeutic alliance, allowing the individual to gradually lower their emotional defenses and engage in vulnerability.

Another crucial aspect of therapeutic intervention for avoidant attachment is to help individuals develop greater self-awareness and insight into their attachment-related behaviors. Through explorative techniques such as reflective listening, guided introspection, and journaling exercises, individuals can begin to recognize the underlying emotional dynamics fueling their avoidance tendencies.

Cognitive-behavioral approaches are instrumental in challenging and restructuring maladaptive thought patterns and beliefs that underpin avoidant attachment. By identifying and reframing negative cognitive schemas, individuals can work towards reconfiguring their relational outlook and fostering more adaptive coping strategies.

Interpersonal therapy is also valuable in addressing avoidant attachment, as it focuses on enhancing communication skills, empathy, and emotional expression within relationships. Therapists guide individuals in managing their interpersonal difficulties and supporting them in establishing healthier and more fulfilling connections with others.

A holistic approach encompassing mindfulness-based practices, emotion regulation techniques, and somatic experiencing can foster embodied healing and integration, helping individuals connect with their emotional experiences and approach intimacy with greater openness and authenticity.

Avoidant Attachment Patterns Across Different Contexts

1. Developmental Origins and Environmental Influences:

As we know, attachment theory posits that the development of avoidant attachment patterns can be influenced by various factors during a person's formative years. These formative years typically encompass early childhood, when individuals are most susceptible to environmental influences that shape their attachment styles. One pivotal factor in the development of avoidant attachment is the quality of the caregiving environment. Research suggests that children who experience consistent neglect or emotional unavailability from their primary caregivers may be more likely to develop avoidant attachment patterns. The lack of responsive and nurturing interactions during critical developmental stages can lead to the internalization of self-reliance and emotional suppression as coping mechanisms. Additionally, insecure attachment in caregivers, particularly dismissive or fearful-avoidant attachment styles, may contribute to the transmission of avoidant tendencies to their children. Furthermore, broader environmental factors such as socio-economic status, cultural norms, and societal support systems play a role in shaping the developmental origins of avoidant attachment. Socio-economic disparities, limited access to resources, and familial stressors can create an environment that hinders the formation of secure attachments, potentially leading to the emergence of avoidant patterns. Cultural attitudes toward emotional expression and individualism versus collectivism also impact the formation of avoidant attachment, as they influence parenting practices and familial dynamics. Moreover, societal support systems, including the availability of mental health resources and community interventions, can mitigate or exacerbate the risk of developing avoidant attachment patterns. Understanding the developmental origins and environmental influences of avoidant attachment is crucial in addressing these patterns across different contexts. By recognizing the multifaceted nature of these influences, it becomes possible to implement targeted interventions and support structures to promote secure attachment and psychological well-being in individuals affected by avoidant attachment.

2. Psychological Characteristics and Behavioral Indicators:

Individuals with avoidant attachment tendencies often exhibit emotional suppression, reluctance to seek comfort from others, and a strong emphasis on self-reliance. These individuals may prioritize independence and autonomy, displaying an aversion to dependency or closeness in interpersonal relationships. Consequently, they may struggle to express vulnerability or openly communicate their feelings, leading to emotional distancing and detachment as protective mechanisms.

In addition to these psychological traits, behavioral indicators of avoidant attachment can be observed through specific interaction patterns and coping mechanisms. Avoidant individuals may demonstrate a preference for maintaining emotional distance in social interactions, exhibiting limited emotional responsiveness and a tendency to withdraw when faced with intimacy or perceived emotional demands. Furthermore, they may rely on avoidance strategies such as minimizing the significance of close relationships, emphasizing self-sufficiency, or engaging in compartmentalization to cope with relational stressors. This behavioral repertoire often stems from early experiences of emotional neglect or inconsistent caregiving, shaping adaptive strategies that prioritize emotional self-preservation.

The impact of avoidant attachment on cognitive processes and self-perception is noteworthy. Individuals with avoidant attachment patterns may develop internalized beliefs centered on distrust of others' motives, skepticism toward emotional intimacy, and a guarded approach to social interactions. These cognitive schemas contribute to a heightened vigilance for potential threats in relationships and a persistent sense of emotional vigilance. As a result, their perceptions of social support and attachment figures may be filtered through a lens of cautious skepticism, predisposing them to interpret benign behaviors as indicators of potential abandonment or rejection.

3. Adolescent Adaptation and Social Functioning:

During adolescence, individuals with avoidant attachment patterns often experience distinct challenges in their social functioning and adaptation to various life situations. This critical developmental stage marks the transition from childhood to adulthood, where peer relationships and social interactions play a pivotal role in shaping one's identity and emotional well-being. Adolescents with avoidant attachment may demonstrate guarded behavior towards establishing close friendships or intimate relationships. As a result, they may struggle with feelings of isolation and alienation, as their reluctance to seek emotional support can lead to difficulties in managing the complex social dynamics prevalent during this period. Furthermore, adolescents with avoidant attachment may exhibit an aversion to vulnerability, making it challenging for them to express their emotions and connect with peers on a deeper level. Such tendencies can contribute to a limited support network and hinder the development of crucial social skills necessary for adaptive functioning. In educational settings, adolescents with avoidant attachment may display disengagement or defiance, impacting their academic performance and relationships with teachers and peers. Moreover, these individuals may struggle with authority figures and resist seeking help when faced with academic or personal challenges. This resolute self-reliance, while seemingly independent, can impede their ability to seek guidance and collaborate effectively within the school environment. Additionally, the prevalence of social media and digital communication platforms further complicates the social landscape for adolescents with avoidant attachment, as the pressure to project an idealized image can exacerbate their fear of rejection and inadequacy. Consequently, these adolescents may find it daunting to engage in virtual social interactions, leading to increased feelings of estrangement and disconnection. Understanding the impact of avoidant attachment on adolescent adaptation is crucial for educators, mental health professionals, and caregivers to provide targeted support and interventions that promote resilience and social integration. By addressing these challenges early on, adolescents with avoidant attachment can develop healthier coping strategies, foster meaningful connections, and cultivate a sense of belonging within their social milieu.

4. Adult Relationships and Emotional Intimacy Challenges:

The core characteristics of avoidance, such as emotional withdrawal, reluctance to trust, and discomfort with emotional closeness, can profoundly impact the dynamics of adult relationships. In romantic partnerships, individuals with avoidant attachment may struggle to engage in deep emotional connection, express vulnerability, or provide consistent support to their partners. This can lead to a sense of emotional distance and dissatisfaction within the relationship for both parties. Furthermore, individuals with avoidant attachment may exhibit a tendency to prioritize independence and self-reliance, which can create barriers to fostering mutual interdependence and intimacy. As a result, these individuals may find themselves caught in a cycle of pushing others away while simultaneously longing for validation and connection. These challenges in adult relationships are often rooted in early experiences of emotional neglect, inconsistent caregiving, or trauma, which have shaped their attachment orientations. Moreover, the fear of rejection and psychological defenses developed in response to past relational wounds can manifest as defensive behaviors and emotional detachment in their current adult relationships. Recognizing and addressing these patterns is crucial for individuals with avoidant attachment to embark on a journey of personal growth and relational healing. Engaging in therapy or self-reflective practices can provide the opportunity for individuals to explore and understand the underlying roots of their avoidant tendencies, cultivate greater self-awareness, and develop healthier strategies for managing emotional intimacy. By acknowledging the impact of early attachment experiences and actively challenging maladaptive coping mechanisms, individuals with avoidant attachment can gradually learn to integrate vulnerability, empathy, and intimacy into their adult relationships.

5. Avoidant Behaviors in the Workplace:

In the context of occupational settings, the manifestation of avoidant attachment behaviors can significantly impact an individual's performance, interactions, and overall well-being. Individuals exhibiting avoidant attachment patterns may display reluctance to seek support from colleagues or supervisors, often preferring independent work and minimal interaction. This preference for autonomy could be perceived as a positive attribute in some roles; however, in collaborative environments, it may lead to challenges in teamwork, communication, and the establishment of cohesive relationships. Such individuals may also struggle with expressing vulnerability or admitting mistakes, which can hinder personal and professional growth. Additionally, the inherent discomfort with emotional intimacy may translate into difficulties in providing and receiving constructive feedback, ultimately affecting productivity and the quality of work. It is crucial for organizational leaders and human resources professionals to recognize and understand these behaviors to create supportive and inclusive work environments. Moreover, interventions such as mentorship programs, training on effective communication and conflict resolution, and promoting psychological safety can help individuals with avoidant attachment styles manage workplace dynamics more effectively. Recognizing the value of diverse attachment styles in the workplace, organizations can foster an environment that accommodates varying communication and collaboration preferences, thereby maximizing the potential of all employees. Beyond the individual level, the influence of avoidant attachment on leadership styles and decision-making processes within organizational structures warrants exploration. Understanding how avoidant individuals respond to authority, manage responsibilities, and engage with power dynamics can offer insights into enhancing leadership effectiveness and team dynamics.

6. Cross-cultural Perspectives on Avoidant Attachment:

Cultural variations can significantly impact the expression and perception of avoidance in relationships and interpersonal interactions. Research has shown that while the concept of avoidant attachment is universal, its manifestation and implications may vary widely across cultures.

One significant aspect to consider is the role of collectivism versus individualism in shaping attachment behaviors. Cultures that prioritize collectivist values often emphasize interconnectedness, interdependence, and harmonious relationships within the community. In such contexts, individuals with avoidant attachment tendencies may face distinct challenges as their inclination towards emotional self-reliance and detachment might conflict with the communal expectations of closeness and mutual support. On the other hand, in individualistic cultures that prioritize autonomy and personal achievement, the expression of avoidant attachment may be more culturally congruent, albeit with potential repercussions on intimate relationships and emotional fulfillment.

Contextual factors such as family structure, societal norms around gender roles, and traditions of emotional expression also contribute to the shaping of avoidant attachment across diverse cultures. For instance, cultural attitudes towards emotional vulnerability, self-disclosure, and intimacy can directly influence how avoidant attachment is perceived and managed within various cultural settings. This highlights the need to approach avoidant attachment from a culturally sensitive lens, acknowledging the nuanced interplay between individual dispositions and cultural contexts.

Additionally, researchers have explored the prevalence and implications of avoidant attachment in cross-cultural romantic relationships, friendships, and professional environments. Comparative studies have illuminated the ways in which cultural diversity impacts the experience and management of avoidant attachment, shedding light on both the challenges and strengths that arise from these differences. Understanding cross-cultural variations in avoidant attachment patterns provides valuable insights for mental health professionals, educators, and policymakers in designing effective interventions and support systems that resonate with diverse cultural perspectives.

7. Clinical Observations and Therapeutic Approaches:

In clinical settings, mental health professionals often encounter individuals exhibiting avoidant attachment behaviors, which can significantly impact their relationships and overall well-being. Through systematic observation and assessment, clinicians can gain valuable insights into the manifestations of avoidant attachment, allowing for tailored therapeutic interventions.

Therapeutic approaches aim to help individuals with avoidant attachment patterns develop healthier and more secure ways of relating to others. Cognitive-behavioral therapy (CBT) has shown promise in addressing maladaptive thought patterns and behaviors associated with avoidant attachment. By identifying and challenging negative beliefs about relationships and intimacy, individuals can gradually learn to form more positive and fulfilling connections.

Additionally, attachment-based interventions focus on promoting emotional regulation and building trust in interpersonal interactions. These approaches often incorporate elements of mindfulness and emotion-focused techniques to help individuals explore and understand their underlying attachment-related fears and defenses. Through gradual exposure and processing of past relational experiences, therapy aims to facilitate a greater sense of security and comfort in forming close bonds.

Psychodynamic therapies delve into the exploration of early attachment experiences and their impact on current relationship dynamics. By exploring unconscious relational patterns and unresolved attachment-related conflicts, individuals can gain insight into the origins of their avoidant tendencies and work towards resolving internal conflicts. The therapeutic relationship itself serves as a crucial arena for experiencing and reworking problematic attachment dynamics.

In clinical practice, it is essential for mental health professionals to approach avoidant attachment with sensitivity and empathy, recognizing the deeply ingrained fears and coping strategies that shape individuals' relational behaviors. Creating a safe and nonjudgmental space for clients to explore their attachment patterns is foundational to the therapeutic process. Additionally, collaborative goal-setting and ongoing feedback ensure that therapeutic interventions are aligned with the unique needs and goals of each individual.

Comparative Analysis of Attachment Styles

1. Core Characteristics Shared Across Attachment Styles:

When examining attachment styles across individuals, it becomes evident that there are fundamental core characteristics that tend to be shared across these different styles. One of the most salient core characteristics is the human need for social connection and the formation of close, meaningful relationships. Regardless of an individual's specific attachment style, humans universally seek out and value connections with others as a means of finding emotional support, security, and a sense of belonging. This desire for close relationships is a foundational element that underpins the concept of attachment and is prevalent across all attachment styles. Additionally, another core characteristic shared across attachment styles is the impact of early caregiver relationships on subsequent social and emotional development. Research consistently highlights the crucial role of early caregiving experiences in shaping an individual's attachment style and their ability to form and maintain relationships later in life. The quality of interactions with primary caregivers during infancy and early childhood lays the groundwork for the internal working models that influence attachment-related behaviors and attitudes throughout the lifespan. Furthermore, emotional regulation emerges as a central core characteristic shared across attachment styles. Individuals with different attachment patterns may exhibit varying strategies for regulating emotions, but the underlying need to manage and cope with emotional experiences is universal. Effective emotional regulation is essential for managing interpersonal relationships and maintaining psychological well-being, making it a pivotal aspect across attachment styles. Moreover, the perception of safety and security in relationships stands out as a common thread among attachment styles. Regardless of whether an individual leans towards secure, anxious, or avoidant attachment, the fundamental desire for feelings of safety, trust, and comfort within close relationships remains consistent. This foundational need for security drives many of the behaviors and relational dynamics inherent in diverse attachment styles.

2. Differential Developmental Pathways and Influences:

From infancy through adulthood, individuals' attachment styles are shaped by a myriad of factors, including but not limited to, parental caregiving behaviors, cultural norms, and societal influences. Differential development of attachment styles begins during the formative years, where infants establish patterns of interaction with their primary caregivers. The quality of caregiving and responsiveness in the early years provides the foundation for the development of secure, anxious, or avoidant attachment styles.

Conceptual frameworks such as Bowlby's ethological theory and Ainsworth's attachment theory have highlighted the significance of these early experiences in shaping individuals' internal working models and relational behaviors. Furthermore, the influence of familial dynamics, such as parental divorce, loss, or trauma, can significantly impact the developmental trajectories of attachment styles. As individuals transition into childhood and adolescence, the influence of social structures and peer relationships becomes increasingly salient. Peer acceptance, rejection, and bullying experiences can dynamically shape attachment patterns, influencing self-esteem, trust, and emotional regulation. Additionally, the broader socio-cultural context plays a pivotal role in shaping attachment styles. Cultural variations in parenting practices, community support systems, and societal values contribute to the diversity of attachment patterns observed across different populations. For instance, collectivistic cultures may prioritize interdependence and emotional restraint, potentially leading to distinct attachment dynamics compared to individualistic cultures. Moreover, societal changes and technological advancements have introduced new dimensions to the developmental pathways of attachment styles. The pervasive influence of digital media, social networking, and virtual interactions has given rise to novel challenges and opportunities in the formation of attachment bonds. Understanding these diverse developmental pathways and influences is critical for professionals in psychology, education, and healthcare.

3. Attachment Styles in Familial and Social Structures:

Attachment styles not only shape individual behavior and experiences, but also have a profound impact on familial and social structures. Within the family unit, attachment patterns often lay the foundation for the quality of parent-child relationships, influencing the emotional attunement, responsiveness, and overall caregiving approach of parents. Secure attachment in parental relationships is associated with greater emotional security, autonomy, and overall psychosocial well-being in children, while anxious or avoidant attachment may lead to emotional dysregulation, insecurity, and difficulty in forming intimate connections. Furthermore, the intergenerational transmission of attachment styles can perpetuate patterns of secure or insecure attachment across generations within familial structures. Within social structures, attachment styles play a pivotal role in shaping the quality of friendships, romantic relationships, and professional interactions. Individuals with secure attachment tend to establish more fulfilling and trusting bonds, whereas those with insecure attachment may struggle with intimacy, communication, and empathy in their social relationships. Moreover, attachment styles influence the formation of social support networks, coping mechanisms, and resilience in the face of adversity. Understanding the interplay between attachment patterns in familial and social structures provides a comprehensive framework for addressing relational dynamics, conflict resolution, and the cultivation of healthy, supportive environments.

4. Psychological Impacts of Diverse Attachment Patterns:

Research has consistently highlighted the significant correlation between attachment styles and psychological well-being, with secure attachment linked to greater emotional resilience and adaptive coping strategies in the face of adversity. In contrast, individuals with anxious attachment tendencies may experience heightened levels of anxiety, hypervigilance, and a propensity for ruminative thought patterns, which can contribute to difficulties in regulating emotions and managing stress. Similarly, those exhibiting avoidant attachment patterns may display emotional detachment, reluctance to seek support, and an inclination towards dismissiveness of their own needs, leading to challenges in forming and maintaining intimate relationships. Understanding the psychological implications of these diverse attachment patterns is integral to providing effective interventions and support. Furthermore, longitudinal studies have indicated that early attachment experiences can shape cognitive schemas and affective regulation, thus influencing one's self-concept, interpersonal behaviors, and overall psychological adjustment. Moreover, the impact of attachment styles extends beyond individual well-being and permeates into broader societal contexts. For instance, individuals with secure attachment tend to demonstrate greater empathy, prosocial behavior, and more constructive conflict resolution skills, contributing positively to social harmony and community resilience. Conversely, individuals with insecure attachment patterns may be at increased risk of developing maladaptive coping mechanisms, susceptibility to mental health disorders, and perpetuating intergenerational patterns of insecure attachment. Recognizing these psychological impacts underscores the importance of promoting secure attachment in various settings, ranging from parenting practices to therapeutic interventions. Emphasizing the role of mental health professionals and caregivers in fostering secure attachment environments can mitigate the adverse psychological consequences associated with diverse attachment patterns, thereby nurturing emotionally healthy individuals and communities.

5. Cross-Cultural Perspectives on Attachment Styles:

As individuals from diverse cultural backgrounds manage the complexities of human relationships, their attachment experiences are deeply woven into the fabric of their cultural heritage. In exploring cross-cultural perspectives on attachment styles, it becomes evident that cultural contexts significantly shape the construction and manifestation of attachment bonds. Cultural norms regarding emotional expression, familial interdepond ence, and societal expectations play a pivotal role in shaping attachment dynamics. For instance, collectivistic cultures may prioritize interconnectedness and group harmony, fostering attachment patterns that emphasize communal relationships and interdependency. In contrast, individualistic cultures may place greater value on independence and autonomy, influencing attachment styles that lean towards self-reliance and personal agency. Moreover, the exploration of cross-cultural perspectives unveils the interplay between attachment styles and cultural transmission. The transmission of attachment norms and behaviors across generations within specific cultural contexts elucidates the impact of cultural traditions on attachment dynamics. It is essential to recognize the nuanced intercultural variations in attachment styles, as they present implications for therapeutic interventions and support systems. By acknowledging the diversity of attachment experiences across cultures, mental health professionals can tailor interventions that resonate with the cultural and relational frameworks of diverse populations. Furthermore, a deepened understanding of cross-cultural perspectives on attachment styles fosters culturally sensitive assessment and intervention strategies, ensuring that individuals receive effective and relevant support within their cultural contexts. By embracing a cross-cultural lens, researchers and practitioners can enrich their comprehension of attachment processes, contributing to the advancement of inclusive and culturally informed psychological practice. The integration of cross-cultural perspectives in attachment research expands our knowledge of the universality and distinctiveness of attachment phenomena, highlighting the need for a multiplicity of narratives in the study of human attachment.

APPLICATIONS OF THE THEORY IN CLINICAL PSYCHOLOGY

Attachment Theory in Psychotherapy

In psychotherapy, attachment theory provides valuable insights into the dynamics of human relationships and the impact of early attachment experiences on an individual's emotional and psychological well-being. Therapists utilize attachment theory to explore clients' relational patterns, emotional regulation, and interpersonal difficulties, fostering a deeper understanding of their internal working models. This understanding forms the foundation for effective therapeutic interventions and client-centered approaches. Through the lens of attachment theory, therapists can help clients develop more secure attachments, strengthen self-esteem, and improve their overall quality of life.

One key aspect of attachment theory in psychotherapy is the emphasis on creating a safe and supportive therapeutic environment. Therapists aim to establish a secure base for clients, mirroring the secure attachment figures described in attachment theory. By providing a nurturing and empathic space, therapists facilitate the exploration of clients' attachment-related struggles and promote healing and growth. This approach allows clients to process unresolved attachment wounds, develop trust in the therapeutic relationship, and experience corrective emotional experiences. Through a combination of insight-oriented techniques and relational interventions, attachment-focused psychotherapy aims to transform clients' maladaptive attachment patterns and enhance their capacity for intimacy and connection.

Attachment theory informs the selection and implementation of therapeutic modalities. Psychodynamic approaches, such as object relations therapy, draw heavily from attachment theory, emphasizing the influence of early caregiver relationships on the development of the self. Cognitive-behavioral interventions are also tailored to address attachment-related schemas and beliefs, targeting specific cognitive distortions linked to insecure attachments. Integrating these modalities within an attachment-informed framework enhances the efficacy of treatment, allowing therapists to address the root causes of clients' emotional distress and relational challenges.

In addition, attachment-based psychotherapy offers valuable insights into the role of the therapeutic bond in facilitating healing and transformation. Therapists strive to cultivate a secure attachment bond with their clients, modeling healthy relational dynamics and promoting emotional attunement. By demonstrating genuine care, responsiveness, and authenticity, therapists provide clients with a corrective emotional experience that counteracts previous attachment-related injuries. This reparative process fosters the development of secure internal working models and empowers clients to form healthier relationships outside the therapeutic setting.

Assessment Tools and Methods

Assessment is a fundamental aspect of applying attachment theory in clinical psychology. It involves the systematic evaluation of an individual's attachment patterns and history to inform treatment planning and intervention strategies. Various tools and methods are utilized to assess attachment, including self-report measures, structured interviews, and observational assessments. Self-report measures such as the Adult Attachment Interview (AAI) and self-administered questionnaires provide insights into an individual's internal working models of attachment and their perceptions of relationships.

Structured interviews, often conducted by trained clinicians, allow for a deeper exploration of attachment-related experiences, providing valuable data for understanding the individual's attachment style and its impact on their psychological well-being. Additionally, observational assessments, such as the Strange Situation Procedure for children or the Adult Attachment Projective Picture System for adults, offer a glimpse into attachment behaviors in controlled settings, allowing for the identification of attachment patterns.

In addition to these standardized tools, clinicians may also employ other methods, including narrative analysis of life stories, assessment of nonverbal behavior, and exploration of family dynamics. Integrating information from multiple sources can offer a comprehensive understanding of an individual's attachment history and current relational patterns.

When conducting assessments, it is essential for clinicians to consider cultural factors that may influence attachment experiences and expressions. Cultural sensitivity and awareness are crucial when interpreting assessment results to avoid misinterpretation or biased conclusions. Furthermore, an interdisciplinary approach, involving collaboration with professionals from diverse backgrounds, can enrich the assessment process and ensure that the complexity of attachment dynamics is thoroughly understood and addressed.

Effective assessment also requires a thorough understanding of attachment theory and its relevance to clinical practice. Clinicians need to be familiar with the various attachment classifications, including secure, anxious-ambivalent, avoidant, and disorganized, and recognize their manifestations across different developmental stages and within diverse relational contexts. By in tegrating theoretical knowledge with practical skills, clinicians can accurately assess attachment patterns and tailor interventions accordingly.

The assessment phase not only provides valuable diagnostic information but also establishes a foundation for formulating personalized treatment plans. It allows clinicians to identify specific goals for therapy, anticipate potential challenges related to attachment issues, and determine the most appropriate therapeutic approaches. This targeted approach enhances the effectiveness of interventions and promotes positive outcomes in clinical settings.

Addressing Attachment Disorders

Assessment of attachment disorders typically involves utilizing a combination of standardized measures, clinical interviews, and behavioral observations to gain insight into an individual's attachment patterns and underlying psychological difficulties. Proficient clinicians are attuned to recognizing symptoms such as indiscriminate sociability, issues with trust and intimacy, and overly controlling or dissociative behaviors that may signify attachment-related concerns. By employing validated assessment tools such as the Strange Situation Procedure and Adult Attachment Interviews, clinicians can gather valuable information to guide treatment planning and intervention selection.

In formulating interventions for attachment disorders, clinicians draw from various therapeutic modalities, including but not limited to attachment-based psychotherapy, cognitive-behavioral approaches, and trauma-informed care. The goals of intervention encompass fostering secure attachment representations, promoting emotional attunement between clients and caregivers, and addressing underlying trauma or relational ruptures that contribute to attachment difficulties. Techniques such as mindfulness-based interventions, emotion-focused therapy, and narrative restructuring often prove beneficial in helping individuals reframe their internal working models and cultivate more adaptive patterns of relating.

Addressing attachment disorders necessitates a careful consideration of ethical principles, particularly in cases involving vulnerable populations such as children and individuals with severe attachment disturbances. Clinicians prioritize informed consent, confidentiality, and cultural sensitivity while managing the complexities of attachment-focused treatments, ensuring that therapeutic endeavors align with the best interests of clients and adhere to professional guidelines.

Interventions for Adults with Insecure Attachments

Individuals with insecure attachment patterns often face significant challenges in forming and maintaining healthy relationships. As such, interventions for adults with insecure attachments aim to address these difficulties and promote relational well-being. Therapeutic approaches commonly used in addressing insecure attachment include cognitive-behavioral therapy (CBT), psychodynamic therapy, and attachment-based interventions. These interventions focus on exploring the individual's attachment history, identifying maladaptive patterns of relating, and fostering healthier interpersonal connections. CBT techniques help individuals recognize and challenge negative thought patterns and behaviors that stem from their attachment experiences. Psychodynamic therapy delves into the unconscious influences of early attachment relationships on current behavior and emotions, facilitating a deeper understanding of one's attachment style. Attachment-based interventions, on the other hand, emphasize creating a secure base for clients to explore and process their attachment-related struggles within the therapeutic relationship. Furthermore, mindfulness-based interventions have shown promise in promoting secure attachment by enhancing self-awareness and emotional regulation. Additionally, group therapy settings provide a supportive environment for individuals with insecure attachments to connect with others who share similar experiences, reducing feelings of isolation and stigma. The incorporation of mindfulness practices and group dynamics can complement individual therapy in addressing the multifaceted nature of insecure attachment. Moreover, addressing unresolved trauma or loss that may contribute to insecure attachment is crucial in interventions for adults. Therapists may utilize trauma-focused interventions such as Eye Movement Desensitization and Reprocessing (EMDR) and narrative exposure therapy to process past experiences and alleviate their impact on attachment patterns. Promoting self-compassion and self-care practices is also integral in helping adults with insecure attachments develop a more positive self-image and enhance their capacity for intimacy. It is essential for therapists to approach interventions for adults with insecure attachments with sensitivity and empathy, considering the deep-seated emotional challenges these individuals may experience.

Application in Family Therapy Contexts

Family therapy is an essential avenue for applying attachment theory, as it allows for a comprehensive exploration of attachment dynamics within the family unit. By understanding how individual attachment patterns interact and influence each other within the family context, therapists can address relational challenges and promote healthier attachment bonds. In family therapy, the focus is not only on the individual's attachment style but also on the interplay of attachment patterns between family members. This approach acknowledges that the family system plays a pivotal role in shaping and reinforcing attachment behaviors and beliefs.

One key aspect of applying attachment theory in family therapy is the identification of attachment hierarchies within the family structure. Therapists explore the attachment bonds between parents and children, between siblings, and between each parent and their children. Understanding these hierarchies provides valuable insights into power dynamics, emotional closeness, and potential conflicts within the family. It also allows for the development of targeted interventions to strengthen secure attachments and address insecure or disorganized attachments.

Another important facet of applying attachment theory in family therapy is the emphasis on creating a secure and supportive environment for exploring attachment-related issues. Therapists facilitate open communication, empathy, and validation within the family sessions to promote emotional attunement and repair ruptures in attachment bonds. This process helps family members develop a deeper understanding of their attachment dynamics and fosters a sense of safety and trust within the therapeutic space.

Family therapists use attachment theory to guide interventions aimed at promoting healthy parent-child relationships and fostering secure attachment in childhood. This may involve providing parents with guidance on responsive and sensitive caregiving, teaching them about the impact of their own attachment history on parenting, and helping them develop strategies to meet their children's attachment needs effectively. Additionally, family therapy interventions incorporate elements of play therapy and narrative approaches to engage children in exploring and expressing their attachment experiences within the family context.

Childhood Interventions and Parenting Approaches

Childhood interventions guided by attachment theory focus on promoting healthy parent-child relationships, addressing attachment disruptions, and supporting secure attachments in early development. Parenting approaches rooted in attachment theory emphasize the importance of sensitive and responsive caregiving to foster secure attachment bonds. Through a combination of psychoeducation, practical strategies, and therapeutic interventions, clinicians work with caregivers to enhance their understanding of child behavior, emotions, and developmental needs within the attachment framework.

Attachment-based parenting interventions involve educating parents about the impact of their interactions on their child's emotional regulation, social development, and overall well-being. This includes promoting attunement to the child's cues, creating a nurturing and predictable environment, and facilitating secure base provision to encourage exploration and autonomy. Clinicians collaborate with parents to identify and address potential attachment difficulties, such as disorganized or ambivalent attachment patterns, through structured interventions that aim to promote greater emotional security and trust between the child and the caregiver.

In clinical practice, childhood interventions also extend to supporting caregivers in managing challenging behaviors, managing separation anxiety, and promoting healthy boundaries within the parent-child relationship. Therapeutic techniques, including play therapy, art therapy, and narrative approaches, are utilized to help children express their thoughts and feelings while enhancing the parent-child bond. Furthermore, clinicians integrate evidence-based parenting programs, such as Circle of Security and Parent-Child Interaction Therapy (PCIT), to provide comprehensive support for both the child and the caregiver.

Parenting approaches informed by attachment theory underscore the significance of sensitivity, warmth, and attunement in fostering secure attachments. By empowering parents with knowledge and skills grounded in attachment principles, clinicians play a crucial role in improving the quality of parent-child interactions and the long-term emotional well-being of children.

Use in Treatment of Trauma and Post-Traumatic Stress Disorder

Treatment of trauma and post-traumatic stress disorder (PTSD) is a critical area where attachment theory plays a significant role. When individuals experience traumatic events, their attachment patterns may influence their response to the trauma and their ability to cope with its aftermath.

One key aspect is recognizing the impact of early attachment experiences on the individual's response to trauma. Those with secure attachments may demonstrate greater resilience and coping mechanisms when facing trauma, while those with insecure attachments could potentially experience more severe symptoms of PTSD. Understanding this link allows clinicians to tailor interventions to address specific attachment-related vulnerabilities.

In therapy, establishing a secure therapeutic alliance is crucial for individuals with trauma or PTSD. Utilizing attachment theory, therapists can create a safe and supportive environment that mirrors the secure base concept. By providing a trusting relationship, therapists enable clients to explore and process traumatic experiences within a secure framework, fostering healing and recovery.

Attachment-focused interventions such as strengthening reflective functioning and internal working models can aid in processing traumatic memories and regulating overwhelming emotions. Helping individuals develop a coherent narrative of their traumatic experiences within the context of their attachment history promotes integration and resolution of the trauma. By addressing attachment-related fears and insecurities, therapists can empower clients to develop healthier coping strategies and diminish PTSD symptoms.

Intersecting attachment theory with evidence-based trauma treatments like cognitive-behavioral therapy (CBT) and eye movement desensitization and reprocessing (EMDR) offers a comprehensive approach to addressing trauma and PTSD. Integrating attachment perspectives into these established modalities enhances the understanding of clients' responses and facilitates more tailored and effective interventions. For instance, incorporating attachment-informed techniques into exposure therapies can promote a sense of safety and trust during the reprocessing of traumatic memories, thus improving treatment outcomes.

Finally, it's essential to pay attention to the broader systemic factors that may impact an individual's attachment dynamics and trauma recovery, including family relationships and social support networks. Understanding the interplay between attachment patterns and systemic influences can guide clinicians in developing holistic treatment plans that address both the individual and relational aspects of trauma and PTSD.

The Integration of Attachment Theory with Other Therapeutic Models

In the field of clinical psychology, the integration of attachment theory with other therapeutic models has garnered significant attention and research interest. By blending the principles of attachment theory with established therapeutic approaches, clinicians can enhance treatment outcomes for a broad range of psychological issues. One prominent example of this integration is the amalgamation of attachment theory with cognitive-behavioral therapy (CBT), a widely utilized modality in the treatment of various mental health concerns.

The integration of attachment theory and CBT capitalizes on the strengths of both frameworks. While CBT primarily focuses on identifying and modifying maladaptive thought patterns and behaviors, an understanding of attachment dynamics provides crucial insights into the development and maintenance of these cognitive and behavioral patterns. For instance, a person with anxious attachment tendencies may exhibit cognitive distortions related to fear of abandonment or unworthiness, which can be effectively addressed within the CBT framework by exploring underlying attachment-related triggers and beliefs.

Integrating attachment theory with humanistic approaches such as person-centered therapy emphasizes the significance of creating a supportive and empathic therapeutic alliance that mirrors secure attachment experiences. By infusing person-centered techniques with attachment-informed interventions, therapists can foster a climate of acceptance, validation, and attunement, crucial components for facilitating the client's exploration of attachment-related themes and emotional vulnerabilities.

The incorporation of attachment theory into psychodynamic therapies enriches the understanding of unconscious relational patterns and early attachment experiences that shape intra-psychic dynamics. This integration allows for a comprehensive exploration of how early attachment experiences contribute to the formation of defense mechanisms, transference dynamics, and internal working models. Consequently, therapists can work collaboratively with clients to process unresolved attachment-related emotions and conflicts within the context of the therapeutic relationship, promoting healing and personal growth.

Additionally, emerging integrative models, such as emotionally focused therapy (EFT), have embraced attachment theory as a foundational framework for understanding and addressing couples' dynamics and individual emotional regulation. By integrating EFT with attachment theory, clinicians can offer nuanced interventions that directly target attachment-related insecurities and promote secure bonding within couples, thereby fostering greater relational satisfaction and resilience.

Ultimately, the integration of attachment theory with diverse therapeutic models represents a progressive step towards a more holistic and nuanced understanding of human functioning and distress. It underscores the importance of considering attachment dynamics in the conceptualization and treatment of psychological difficulties, paving the way for innovative and effective clinical interventions.

Ethical Considerations and Challenges in Clinical Practice

Integrating attachment theory with other therapeutic models presents various ethical considerations and challenges that clinicians must address in clinical practice. One challenge arises from the potential for conflicting principles and techniques between attachment theory and other therapeutic approaches. Clinicians must carefully consider how to integrate these diverse frameworks without compromising ethical standards or causing confusion for clients. Another ethical consideration involves the informed consent process. When incorporating attachment theory into therapy, clinicians must ensure that clients fully understand the implications, limitations, and potential risks of integrating this approach into their treatment. This requires clear communication and transparency regarding the goals, methods, and possible outcomes associated with utilizing attachment theory in clinical practice. Furthermore, confidentiality issues may arise when working with attachment-related content, particularly in cases where sensitive family dynamics and personal histories are explored. Clinicians must uphold strict confidentiality guidelines while also recognizing the importance of addressing attachment-related issues within a familial context. Additionally, power differentials within the therapeutic relationship can present ethical challenges. Clinicians need to be mindful of their influence and authority, especially when exploring sensitive attachment-related material, to ensure that clients feel empowered and respected throughout the therapeutic process. Furthermore, the cultural sensitivity of attachment theory and its applications in clinical practice cannot be overlooked. Clinicians must actively consider the cultural backgrounds, beliefs, and values of their clients while integrating attachment theory, avoiding the imposition of ethnocentric views or assumptions. Understanding and respecting cultural diversity is essential in maintaining ethical standards and promoting effective therapeutic outcomes. Finally, the ongoing evaluation of the effectiveness and appropriateness of integrating attachment theory into clinical practice is imperative. Clinicians must engage in regular self-assessment, seek supervision, and stay attuned to emerging research to ensure that their use of attachment theory aligns with best practices and ethical guidelines. Managing these ethical considerations and challenges demands a thoughtful and conscientious approach, ultimately contributing to the ethical and effective application of attachment theory within clinical psychology.

CRITIQUES AND COUNTERARGUMENTS

Methodological Limitations in Attachment Research

Attachment research has significantly contributed to our understanding of human relationships, yet it is important to critically assess its methodological foundation. One of the primary limitations in attachment research lies in the reliance on self-report measures and retrospective data. While these methods provide valuable insights into individuals' perceptions and interpretations of their attachment experiences, they are subject to biases, memory distortions, and social desirability effects. Additionally, the use of self-reports may not fully capture the complexity of attachment dynamics and could be influenced by individual differences in communication styles and emotional expressiveness.

Another methodological challenge is the reliance on homogenous samples, particularly in early attachment studies. Many of the seminal studies in attachment theory were conducted with middle-class, Caucasian families, leading to concerns about the generalizability of findings across diverse cultural and socio-economic contexts. This limitation raises questions about the universality of attachment patterns and the extent to which they are shaped by cultural norms and contextual factors.

Longitudinal studies in attachment research often encounter difficulties in maintaining participant retention over extended periods. Attrition rates can affect the reliability and validity of longitudinal data, potentially biasing conclusions about the stability and continuity of attachment patterns across development. Moreover, ethical considerations related to long-term follow-up and potential psychological harm to participants pose challenges to implementing rigorous longitudinal designs.

In addition to these methodological limitations, there is a need for greater integration of qualitative approaches in attachment research. Qualitative methods such as narrative analysis, ethnographic observations, and in-depth interviews can offer rich, contextualized accounts of attachment experiences that complement quantitative assessments. By incorporating diverse methodological approaches, researchers can gain a more comprehensive understanding of the complexities inherent in attachment processes and better capture the subjective meanings individuals attribute to their attachment relationships.

Addressing these methodological limitations requires a concerted effort to diversify sampling strategies, implement innovative assessment tools, and adopt interdisciplinary perspectives. Overcoming these challenges is essential for advancing attachment research and developing more nuanced theoretical frameworks that account for the intricacies of human attachment across diverse contexts and populations.

Theoretical Criticisms: Broadening the Scope

In expanding the critique of attachment theory, it is essential to consider the theoretical criticisms that have emerged over time. One of the primary areas of concern pertains to the narrow scope of attachment theory in understanding human relationships. Critics argue that attachment theory predominantly focuses on the parent-child dyad and may not adequately account for other significant relationships, such as those with siblings, peers, or extended family members. Moreover, the theory's emphasis on caregiver-child interactions potentially overlooks the influence of broader social networks, including the role of teachers, mentors, and community support systems in facilitating healthy development.

The traditional emphasis on maternal caregiving has been criticized for its neglect of paternal and alternate caregiving roles. Critics contend that attachment theory's historical grounding in a patriarchal societal structure may have perpetuated gender biases, limiting the exploration of diverse caregiving models and their impact on attachment dynamics. This limitation may hinder a comprehensive understanding of attachment processes within varied family structures and across cultural contexts.

Additionally, some scholars argue that attachment theory's reliance on ethological and evolutionary frameworks may oversimplify the complexities of human attachment dynamics. The exclusive focus on biological instincts and the adaptive function of attachment behaviors may neglect the significance of cognitive, emotional, and socio-cultural aspects in shaping attachment experiences. By broadening the theoretical framework to encompass multidimensional influences, including individual differences, interpersonal dynamics, and socio-historical contexts, a more nuanced understanding of attachment phenomena can be cultivated.

It is imperative to acknowledge these theoretical criticisms, as they prompt scholars and practitioners to adopt a more inclusive and comprehensive perspective on attachment processes. By broadening the scope of inquiry, researchers can delve into the complex interplay of various relational dynamics, social factors, and cultural nuances that shape human attachment throughout the lifespan. Embracing a broader theoretical framework not only enriches our comprehension of attachment phenomena but also empowers us to recognize and address the diversity of human experiences and relationships.

Cultural Biases in Attachment Theory

Attachment theory, based predominantly on research conducted in Western cultures, has been critiqued for its cultural biases. The theory's original formulation by John Bowlby and subsequent research by Mary Ainsworth primarily focused on attachment behaviors observed in the United States and Europe. This limited cultural scope raises concerns about the universality of attachment classifications and the applicability of the theory to diverse cultural contexts. Critics argue that the emphasis on individualistic ideals in Western societies may not fully capture the complexities of attachment dynamics in collectivistic cultures.

Studies have shown that the traditional Strange Situation procedure, often used to assess attachment patterns, may not accurately reflect attachment dynamics in non-Western cultures. The reliance on separation and reunion scenarios as indicators of attachment security may not align with cultural norms where caregivers and children interact differently. Additionally, the assumption that secure attachment is the optimal standard may be influenced by Western cultural values, potentially neglecting the variability of healthy attachment practices across different cultural settings.

Cultural differences in caregiving practices, such as the role of extended family members or communal child-rearing, may challenge the uniformity of attachment expectations. For instance, in some indigenous cultures, the concept of multiple attachment figures and interdependence within social networks could diverge from the Western ideal of a primary caregiver-child bond. These variations in caregiving dynamics necessitate a critical examination of how attachment theory aligns with cultural realities and challenges ethnocentric interpretations.

The Reevaluation of Secure Attachment Standards

Secure attachment has long been considered the gold standard in attachment theory, representing a healthy and optimal caregiving environment that fosters a child's emotional well-being and development. However, as our understanding of cultural diversity and individual differences has expanded, there has been a growing call to reevaluate the universal application of secure attachment standards.

One of the primary challenges in assessing secure attachment lies in the potential bias towards Western, middle-class norms and values. The original research on attachment theory was predominantly conducted in Western societies, which may not fully capture the diverse range of caregiving practices and familial structures present in non-Western cultures. As such, the criteria for identifying secure attachment may inadvertently favor certain cultural norms while marginalizing others, leading to an incomplete and potentially biased understanding of what constitutes secure attachment.

The assumption of a singular, universally applicable definition of secure attachment fails to acknowledge the wide spectrum of relational dynamics and caregiver-child interactions that can promote emotional security and resilience. This narrow conceptualization overlooks the adaptive strategies and strengths that children from different backgrounds develop within their respective caregiving environments. By reevaluating secure attachment standards, we can move towards a more inclusive and culturally sensitive framework that recognizes and respects the diverse manifestations of healthy attachment across various cultural contexts.

Additionally, the quest to reevaluate secure attachment standards necessitates a critical examination of the inherent relationship between attachment classifications and social privilege. Research has shown that attachment patterns may intersect with socioeconomic factors, systemic inequalities, and historical contexts, influencing the accessibility and manifestation of secure attachment. As such, the traditional benchmarks for secure attachment may inadvertently reflect and perpetuate socio-economic biases, thereby reinforcing existing disparities in access to supportive caregiving resources and opportunities

The Issue of the Universality of Attachment Classifications

Attachment theory has long been regarded as a universal framework for understanding interpersonal relationships, particularly between children and caregivers. However, a growing body of research has raised questions about the universality of attachment classifications proposed by the theory. While the original categorizations of secure, anxious, and avoidant attachment styles have provided valuable insights into early relationship patterns, there is now evidence to suggest that these classifications may not hold true across all cultural contexts and diverse populations. A key consideration in challenging the universality of attachment classifications lies in acknowledging the inherent biases and ethnocentric assumptions that underpin the development of attachment theory. The concept of 'secure attachment' may reflect specific cultural norms and values, leading to a narrow interpretation of what constitutes healthy attachment behaviors. Moreover, studies conducted in non-Western contexts have revealed a broader range of caregiving practices and attachment patterns that do not neatly fit into the established categories. These findings prompt a critical reevaluation of the criteria used to assess attachment classifications and call for a more culturally sensitive approach that recognizes the diversity of attachment experiences worldwide. Additionally, the role of societal structures and environmental influences in shaping attachment dynamics cannot be ignored. Socioeconomic disparities, family structures, and community support systems vary widely across different cultural contexts, influencing the nature of caregiving and the formation of attachment bonds. Thus, challenging the universality of attachment classifications necessitates a holistic examination of the socio-cultural factors that shape attachment experiences. Furthermore, recent research in developmental psychology and anthropology has highlighted the need for inclusivity and representation in constructing attachment frameworks. Diverse voices and perspectives from marginalized communities can provide valuable insights into alternative attachment patterns that may challenge traditional classifications. By considering a broader spectrum of attachment behaviors and relational dynamics, we can move towards a more inclusive and nuanced understanding of human attachment. In doing so, we can bridge the gap between universal principles and culturally specific manifestations of attachment, paving the way for a more comprehensive and adaptive attachment theory.

Psychological Perspectives

In examining attachment theory from psychological perspectives, it becomes evident that diverging viewpoints exist regarding the nature and implications of attachment classifications.

Psychologists bringing various theoretical orientations often interpret and analyze attachment research in contrasting ways, leading to disagreements and debates within the field. For instance, scholars adhering to psychodynamic perspectives may emphasize the impact of early childhood experiences on personality development, highlighting the significance of attachment relationships in shaping an individual's internal working models and relational patterns. In contrast, cognitive psychologists might focus on the cognitive processes involved in attachment, such as the role of schemas and information processing in forming attachment representations.

Behavioral psychologists may scrutinize attachment behaviors through the lens of reinforcement and conditioning, elucidating how attachment bonds are established and maintained through operant and classical conditioning mechanisms. On the other hand, humanistic psychologists may underscore the subjective experiences and self-actualization tendencies within attachment dynamics, emphasizing the importance of empathy, genuineness, and unconditional positive regard in fostering secure attachments.

Additionally, evolutionary psychologists offer an evolutionary perspective on attachment, asserting that attachment behaviors and patterns have evolved as adaptive strategies for survival and reproduction. They posit that different attachment patterns may reflect diverse evolutionary strategies related to caregiving and mating. Within these diverse psychological perspectives, conflicts and discrepancies arise concerning the origins, functions, and developmental outcomes of attachment, thus contributing to a rich tapestry of theoretical discourse and interpretation.

The Role of Environmental and Socioeconomic Factors

Research has increasingly highlighted the influence of external environments on the development and expression of attachment patterns. Socioeconomic status, family dynamics, cultural practices, and societal structures all play pivotal roles in shaping individuals' attachment experiences from infancy through adulthood.

Socioeconomic factors have been found to significantly impact caregiving practices and parental responsiveness, which are fundamental in forming secure attachments. Lower socioeconomic status is often associated with higher levels of stress, limited access to resources, and unstable living conditions, all of which can affect the quality of parent-child interactions and the establishment of secure attachment bonds. Moreover, economic disparities can lead to variations in parenting styles and disciplinary strategies, potentially influencing the formation of attachment patterns.

Environmental factors, including the quality of caregiving environments, exposure to adversity, and access to social support, also contribute to the development of attachment relationships. Children growing up in nurturing and emotionally supportive environments are more likely to develop secure attachment patterns, while those exposed to neglect, abuse, or other adverse experiences may exhibit insecure attachment behaviors. The role of the broader social environment, such as neighborhood safety, community support, and educational opportunities, cannot be overlooked in understanding attachment outcomes.

Cultural norms and practices significantly shape attachment dynamics. Different cultural contexts may prioritize distinct caregiving behaviors, emotional expressions, and relational values, thereby influencing attachment patterns in diverse ways. Recognizing and appreciating the diversity of attachment experiences across cultures is crucial for a comprehensive understanding of attachment dynamics.

The Integration of Alternative Theories and Frameworks

In the ongoing quest to refine and enhance attachment theory, scholars and researchers have increasingly turned their attention to the integration of alternative theories and frameworks. This integrative approach seeks to broaden our understanding of human attachment by incorporating insights from diverse psychological perspectives and theoretical paradigms. One prominent avenue of integration involves the exploration of relational and interpersonal theories, such as object relations theory and social exchange theory.

The inclusion of developmental theories, particularly those focusing on socioemotional development and temperament, offers a more comprehensive view of the multifaceted nature of attachment processes. Understanding how individual differences in temperament and emotional regulation influence attachment behaviors provides a nuanced framework for investigating the intricacies of attachment patterns across diverse populations and contexts.

The field of neuroscience has significantly contributed to the advancement of attachment research by elucidating the neurobiological underpinnings of attachment-related behaviors and emotions. Integrating findings from neurobiological studies into attachment theory not only enriches our understanding of the physiological mechanisms involved in attachment, but also sheds light on the potential impact of early experiences on brain development and subsequent attachment patterns.

Beyond these domains, integrating cultural and existential perspectives is pivotal in fostering a more inclusive and holistic understanding of attachment phenomena. By acknowledging the influence of cultural norms, values, and belief systems on attachment dynamics, researchers can better appreciate the diversity of attachment experiences within various cultural contexts. Additionally, exploring existential dimensions of attachment, such as the search for meaning and security, offers a deeper understanding of how attachment figures into broader existential themes and the human quest for connection and belonging.

Ultimately, the integration of alternative theories and frameworks serves to enrich attachment theory by broadening its scope, promoting interdisciplinary collaboration, and fostering a more nuanced understanding of human attachment across different levels of analysis. As we continue to embrace diverse theoretical perspectives and incorporate multidisciplinary insights, we are poised to advance attachment theory into a more comprehensive, dynamic, and integrative framework that captures the rich tapestry of human attachment experiences.

FUTURE DIRECTIONS & RESEARCH IN ATTACHMENT THEORY

Technological Advancements and Their Impact on Attachment Studies

The landscape of attachment research has been greatly influenced by the advent of technological advancements, revolutionizing the way researchers investigate and understand attachment dynamics. The integration of advanced imaging techniques such as fMRI and EEG has provided unprecedented insights into the neural mechanisms underlying attachment behaviors, shedding light on the interplay between brain activity and social bonding. Furthermore, the development of sophisticated behavioral observation tools and wearable sensors has enabled real-time monitoring of attachment-related behaviors in naturalistic settings, offering a more ecologically valid assessment of attachment processes. Digital platforms and virtual reality simulations have also emerged as promising tools for exploring the influence of social media and online interactions on attachment formation and maintenance in contemporary society.

On the other hand, the utilization of big data analytics and machine learning algorithms has empowered researchers to analyze massive datasets encompassing diverse cultural and demographic samples, allowing for a comprehensive cross-cultural examination of attachment patterns and the identification of universal versus culture-specific elements. Additionally, the integration of genomic research has opened up new avenues for investigating the genetic underpinnings of attachment security and susceptibility to attachment-related psychopathology, yielding valuable insights into the heritability of attachment styles.

In the sphere of intervention and treatment, teletherapy and mobile applications have been harnessed to deliver accessible and personalized support for individuals managing attachment-related challenges, extending the reach of therapeutic interventions beyond traditional clinical settings. These technological innovations hold immense potential for enhancing the efficacy and accessibility of attachment-based interventions, thereby fostering secure attachment relationships and ameliorating attachment-related difficulties.

However, it is pivotal to acknowledge the ethical implications and privacy concerns surrounding the use of technology in attachment research, necessitating a cautious approach to safeguard the confidentiality and well-being of participants. As technology continues to evolve at a rapid pace, researchers must remain vigilant and critically evaluate the impact of these advancements on the authenticity and validity of attachment research findings.

Interdisciplinary Approaches to Attachment Theory

Interdisciplinary approaches to attachment theory have become increasingly essential in advancing our understanding of human attachment across the lifespan. By integrating insights and methodologies from diverse fields such as psychology, neuroscience, sociology, anthropology, and genetics, researchers have been able to gain a more comprehensive perspective on attachment processes.

One of the primary benefits of interdisciplinary collaboration is the opportunity to examine attachment phenomena from multiple vantage points. Psychologists contribute valuable insights into the socioemotional dynamics of attachment, while neuroscientists shed light on the underlying brain mechanisms involved in forming and maintaining attachment bonds. Sociological perspectives help situate attachment within broader social structures and cultural contexts, elucidating the impact of societal norms and values on attachment patterns. The intersection of these disciplines not only enriches our theoretical understanding of attachment but also informs practical interventions and policy initiatives.

Interdisciplinary collaboration fosters innovative research methodologies that transcend the boundaries of traditional disciplinary silos. For instance, the integration of genetic studies with attachment research has enabled investigations into the genetic underpinnings of attachment styles and their implications for mental health outcomes. Similarly, the use of advanced imaging techniques in neuroscience has provided unprecedented insights into the neural correlates of attachment processes, offering compelling evidence for the biological basis of human attachment. Such methodological synergies underscore the transformative potential of interdisciplinary approaches in pushing the frontiers of attachment theory and research.

Interdisciplinary dialogues have spurred critical reflections on the universality of attachment theory and the need for greater cultural inclusivity. By engaging with anthropological perspectives, researchers have begun to unravel the diversity of attachment practices across different societies and the ways in which cultural variations shape attachment dynamics. This expanded cultural lens not only challenges ethnocentric biases in attachment research but also underscores the importance of contextualizing attachment within a global, multicultural framework.

Innovative Methodologies for Analyzing Attachment Patterns

The study of attachment patterns has greatly benefited from innovative methodologies that have expanded our understanding of human relationships. One such methodology involves the use of advanced imaging techniques, such as functional magnetic resonance imaging (fMRI) and positron emission tomography (PET), to investigate the neural underpinnings of attachment-related behaviors. By examining brain activity in response to attachment-related stimuli, researchers can elucidate the neurobiological basis of attachment and its implications for emotional regulation and social bonding. Additionally, advancements in behavioral coding systems and observational methods have provided researchers with more nuanced ways to assess attachment behaviors across various contexts. From microanalytic coding of interactions to automated behavioral tracking using machine learning algorithms, these innovative approaches enable a more comprehensive analysis of attachment dynamics. Moreover, the integration of physiological measures, such as heart rate variability and cortisol levels, has shed light on the psychophysiological aspects of attachment processes, offering a holistic perspective on the interplay between biology and behavior. Furthermore, the burgeoning field of epigenetics has opened new avenues for investigating the intergenerational transmission of attachment patterns. By examining DNA methylation patterns and gene expression related to attachment-relevant genes, researchers are uncovering the molecular mechanisms through which early caregiving experiences impact long-term attachment outcomes. Another groundbreaking development is the application of virtual reality technology to simulate attachment scenarios, providing a controlled yet immersive environment for studying attachment behaviors and their underlying mechanisms. Virtual reality-based paradigms offer unique insights into individuals' responses to attachment-related stressors and provide a platform for interventions aimed at improving attachment security.

Attachment and Neurobiology

Advancements in neuroimaging techniques such as functional magnetic resonance imaging (fMRI) have allowed researchers to explore the neural underpinnings of attachment-related processes. Studies utilizing fMRI have demonstrated that specific brain areas, notably the amygdala and prefrontal cortex, play crucial roles in regulating emotional responses and social bonding, shedding light on the neurological basis of attachment. Furthermore, investigations into the neurochemical substrates of attachment have uncovered the influence of oxytocin, often referred to as the 'love hormone,' and its impact on affiliative behaviors and bonding. Understanding these neurochemical pathways provides valuable insights into the physiological mechanisms that underpin attachment relationships. As we strive to bridge the gap between attachment theory and neurobiology, it is imperative to consider the implications of these interdisciplinary findings. The integration of neurobiological perspectives can offer nuanced explanations for attachment patterns observed across diverse populations and developmental stages. Moreover, this holistic approach has profound implications for clinical interventions, as it opens up avenues for targeted therapeutic strategies informed by a deeper understanding of the neurobiological correlates of attachment-related challenges. However, ethical considerations must accompany the exploration of neurobiological aspects of attachment, emphasizing the need for responsible research practices and the conscientious application of findings in practical settings.

Attachment Theory Beyond Traditional Boundaries

Attachment theory, while traditionally focused on dyadic relationships and the parent-child bond, has seen a significant expansion beyond these conventional boundaries in recent years. This evolution has been driven by a growing recognition of the influence of broader social, cultural, and environmental factors on attachment dynamics. One crucial area of expansion is the exploration of attachment patterns in non-traditional family structures, such as single-parent households, blended families, and same-sex parent families. Understanding how attachment theory operates within these diverse family contexts can provide valuable insights for practitioners and policymakers alike. Another frontier in expanding attachment theory involves its applicability to non-human relationships. Research into attachment behaviors in animal species has shed light on the evolutionary roots of attachment and the universality of attachment principles across species. This interdisciplinary approach has prompted fruitful collaborations between ethologists, psychologists, and neuroscientists, enriching our understanding of attachment processes. Furthermore, globalization and increased mobility have spurred investigations into attachment dynamics in multicultural settings. The impact of migration, acculturation, and transnational relationships on attachment styles and interpersonal bonds has emerged as a pivotal area of inquiry. Studies in this sphere not only contribute to cross-cultural psychology but also offer practical implications for supporting individuals adapting to diverse socio-cultural landscapes. Moreover, as digital communication becomes integral to modern human interactions, researchers are delving into the influence of virtual attachments and technologically-mediated relationships on attachment patterns. This exploration encompasses the examination of online communities, long-distance relationships, and the impact of social media on attachment-related behaviors. Understanding the intersection of technology and attachment is paramount in an era where virtual connectivity shapes significant aspects of human connection. Lastly, the extension of attachment theory to marginalized and vulnerable populations, including individuals with developmental disabilities, trauma survivors, and incarcerated individuals, underscores the potential for attachment theory to inform inclusive and equitable interventions.

Longitudinal Studies and Their Insights into Adult Attachment

By observing individuals over time, researchers can discern patterns of stability and change in attachment styles, providing a comprehensive understanding of adult attachment dynamics. Longitudinal studies have illuminated the interplay between early caregiving environments and subsequent relationship outcomes, elucidating the continuity or transformation of attachment patterns in adulthood. This longitudinal approach allows researchers to explore the potential influence of life events, such as transitions, trauma, or significant relationships, on the development and adaptation of attachment styles. Furthermore, longitudinal research facilitates the identification of protective factors that contribute to resilience in the face of adversities, offering valuable implications for intervention and support programs. The longitudinal perspective enables the examination of generational transmission of attachment patterns, elucidating how adult caregivers' attachment representations influence their children's attachment security. Additionally, longitudinal studies provide meaningful data on the association between adult attachment and various domains of functioning, including emotional regulation, mental health outcomes, and interpersonal relationships. Such multifaceted insights enhance our comprehension of the far-reaching implications of adult attachment across diverse contexts. Moreover, longitudinal investigations can contribute to the refinement and validation of assessment tools, ensuring that measures accurately capture the nuanced dynamics of adult attachment over time. As research methodologies continue to evolve, longitudinal studies incorporating diverse populations and cultural contexts hold promise in enriching our understanding of the universality and cultural specificity of attachment phenomena. The integration of advanced statistical techniques and innovative measurement approaches further strengthens the reliability and validity of findings from longitudinal research, fostering the accumulation of robust evidence in the field of adult attachment.

Policy Implications and Public Health Applications

The field of attachment theory has significant implications for public policy and the broader sphere of public health. One crucial area of policy implication is in early childhood development and childcare. Research has consistently shown that secure attachment in early childhood serves as a protective factor against a myriad of negative outcomes later in life, including mental health issues, substance abuse, and relationship difficulties. Therefore, policies that support high-quality parental leave, affordable and accessible childcare, and early intervention programs can play a critical role in fostering secure attachments and promoting healthy development among young children.

On the other hand, attachment theory has direct relevance to the healthcare sector, particularly in the spheres of mental health and interpersonal interventions. Understanding an individual's attachment patterns can significantly impact the effectiveness of therapeutic interventions and the design of mental health treatment programs. Integrating attachment-informed practices into clinical settings and mental health policies can enhance the overall quality of care and improve treatment outcomes.

In addition to individual-level interventions, attachment theory also points toward the importance of creating supportive environments within communities and institutions. This has significant implications for public health strategies aimed at addressing social inequalities, supporting vulnerable populations, and preventing adverse childhood experiences. By promoting policies and programs that aim to create nurturing and supportive social environments, policymakers can contribute to improving overall public health outcomes and reducing the prevalence of mental health disorders. Moreover, the incorporation of attachment-informed practices in educational policies can have far-reaching effects on students' socio-emotional development and academic performance. Schools that prioritize strategies aligned with our understanding of attachment needs and patterns are better positioned to support students' holistic development and well-being.

Finally, ethical considerations must be carefully integrated into any policies derived from attachment research. As we develop and implement policies based on attachment theory, it is essential to uphold ethical standards, respect individuals' autonomy, and ensure that interventions are conducted in a manner that prioritizes the well-being of all involved parties. Tackling complex societal issues through attachment-informed policies requires a nuanced and ethical approach that balances the potential benefits with the protection of individuals' rights and dignity.

Ethical Considerations in Future Attachment Research

As the field continues to evolve and expand, it becomes increasingly imperative to uphold ethical standards that prioritize the well-being of study participants and respect their rights. One essential element in the ethical conduct of attachment research involves obtaining informed consent from all individuals involved, including children and vulnerable populations. Researchers must ensure that participants fully comprehend the nature of the study, its potential risks, and benefits before voluntarily agreeing to take part. Moreover, special attention should be given to protecting the anonymity and confidentiality of participants, particularly when exploring sensitive topics related to attachment dynamics and interpersonal relationships. This entails implementing stringent data security measures and utilizing de-identification techniques to safeguard the privacy of individuals who contribute to research initiatives.

As attachment theory delves into diverse cultural contexts and societal norms, researchers must address the complexities of cross-cultural ethics with sensitivity and respect. Acknowledging and addressing power differentials, historical imbalances, and colonial legacies is fundamental in fostering equitable and ethical research practices. Collaborating with local communities, engaging in participatory approaches, and integrating indigenous perspectives can enrich the ethical fabric of attachment research by ensuring that investigations are culturally appropriate and beneficial for all stakeholders involved.

In addition to respecting the rights of participants, ethical considerations in future attachment research also extend to the dissemination and utilization of findings. Researchers bear the responsibility of presenting their results accurately and transparently, while refraining from sensationalizing or misrepresenting data to garner attention. Moreover, they must strive to contribute to the broader scientific community by sharing insights, methodologies, and potential limitations of their studies. Open dialogue and collaboration within the research community can fortify ethical principles and promote a culture of accountability and integrity in attachment research.

As technology continues to advance, ethical considerations in attachment research must also address the implications of utilizing cutting-edge tools such as neuroimaging and genetic analysis. It is crucial to weigh the ethical implications of storing and interpreting sensitive biological and neurological data, ensuring that such information is handled ethically, securely, and with the utmost respect for individual autonomy and privacy. Furthermore, ethical frameworks should guide the use of emerging technologies in a manner that prioritizes the well-being of participants and contributes meaningfully to the advancement of attachment theory without compromising ethical standards.

In summary, ethical considerations in future attachment research encompass a broad spectrum of responsibilities, including participant consent, cultural sensitivity, transparency in reporting findings, and ethical use of advancing technologies. Upholding these ethical principles not only safeguards the integrity of research endeavors but also ensures that the well-being and rights of all individuals involved remain at the forefront of attachment research.

BOWLBY'S 50 QUOTES ON ATTACHMENT THEORY

On the Nature of Attachment & Human Bonds

"The propensity to make strong emotional bonds to particular individuals is a basic component of human nature."

"For to have a deep attachment for a person (or a place or thing) is to have taken them as the terminating object of our instinctual responses."

"What cannot be communicated to the mother cannot be communicated to the self."

"I regard the desire to be loved and cared for as being an integral part of human nature throughout adult life."

"Attachment is not a fixed trait; it can be influenced and shaped by later experiences and relationships."

"The attachment system is an integral part of our human nature, influencing our thoughts, behaviors, and emotions throughout our lives."

"Attachment relationships set the stage for a child's emotional and cognitive development, shaping their future experiences and relationships."

"The need for attachment is a fundamental human need, just like the need for food and shelter."

On Early Experience & Lasting Impact

"The lasting effects of early experiences are often underestimated, yet they lay the foundation for a lifetime of emotional well-being."

"Early relationships lay the groundwork for emotional regulation, empathy, and social competence in adulthood."

"A securely attached child will store an internal working model of a responsive, loving, reliable care-giver [...]"

"[...] Conversely, an insecurely attached child may view the world as a dangerous place [...]"

"Children who experience secure attachment are more likely to develop healthy self-esteem, positive relationships, and emotional well-being."

"The quality of early relationships serves as a template for future relationships [...]"

"Attachment is the mechanism by which the infant and young child ensures proximity to his principal caregiver in whatever circumstances he finds himself."

On Secure Base & Exploration

"Life is best organized as a series of daring ventures from a secure base."

"Secure attachment provides a safe haven and a secure base from which individuals can explore the world and develop a sense of self."

"Secure attachment promotes a sense of trust and confidence in the world [...]"

"Responsive caregiving promotes secure attachment, providing children with a solid foundation for healthy development."

"Emotional availability and responsiveness of caregivers are crucial for establishing secure attachment bonds."

On Emotional Regulation & Resilience

"Secure attachment fosters the development of emotional regulation skills, allowing individuals to cope with stress and regulate their emotions effectively."

"Attachment provides comfort, security, and trust that helps individuals manage life's challenges with greater resilience."

"The human psyche, like human bones, is strongly inclined towards self-healing."

"Thus, in the right place, at the right time, and in right degree, anger is not only appropriate but may be indispensable [...]"

On Separation, Anxiety & Attachment Distress

"For to have a deep attachment for a person is to have taken them as the terminating object of our instinctual responses."

"When a relationship to a special loved person is endangered, we are not only anxious but are usually angry as well..."

"Try to prise a limpet away from its rock and it will cling all the harder."

"Young children deprived of continuous care and attention may suffer long-term effects which persist."

"It is not food or nourishment that determines attachment. Instead, it is the responsiveness of caregivers [...]"

On Internal Working Models & Expectations

"To ascribe feeling is usually to make a prediction about subsequent behavior."

"Attachment relationships contribute to an internal working model of self and others [...]"

"An insecurely attached person may feel intense dependency and fear of rejection [...]"

"The internal working model shapes expectations and patterns of relating across the lifespan."

On Psychoanalysis & Scientific Perspective

"It was regarded as almost outside the proper interest of an analyst to give systematic attention to a person's real experiences."

"All knowledge is conjectural [...] science progresses through new theories coming to replace older ones [...]"

"Whoever may still be skeptical whether knowledge of animal behavior can help our understanding of man can find no support from Freud."

"Now there is nothing unscientific in utilizing, for the interpretation of data, any model that seems promising [...]"

On Maternal Care & Child Development

"If a community values its children, it must cherish its mothers."

"If we value our children, we must cherish their parents."

"Since [...] transitional objects [...] play no special role, a more appropriate term for them would be simply 'substitute objects'."

"At the time of his second birthday [...] a healthy child [...] makes excursions away from his mother, returning before the next [...]"

On Attachment Across the Lifespan

"Attachment needs continue throughout life and are not outgrown."

"All close relationships reflect core attachment experiences formed in early life."

"Attachment influences how we regulate emotions, think about self, and relate to others far beyond childhood."

Miscellaneous Insightful Quotations

"The stark nakedness and simplicity of the conflict with which humanity is oppressed [...]"

"The fact that emotional feeling can be experienced during sleep is a reminder [...]"

"Not only is progress of the overall activity monitored but progress of each bit of it [...]"

"One difficulty of exposition is that each sort of appraisal process [...]"

"Propositions of a genetic and adaptive sort are found throughout this book [...]"

"Thus, appraisal is a complex process in which two main steps can be distinguished [...]"

www.ingramcontent.com/pod-product-compliance
Lightning Source LLC
LaVergne TN
LVHW052325200926
848481LV00002B/671
* 9 7 9 8 2 3 2 0 6 3 8 6 3 *